Discharged Fluid Handling Process

Ville-Roi Pierrechamp

Discharged Fluid Handling Process

First Edition June 2025

Written by Ville-Roi Pierrechamp

TABLE OF CONTENTS

LIST OF TABLES

LIST OF FIGURES

LIST OF SYMBOLS AND ABBREVIATIONS

ANFIS	Adaptive Neuro-Fuzzy Inference System
DAQ	Data Acquisition
DO	Dissolved Oxygen
FAU	Formazin Attenuation Units
HCl	Hydrochloric Acid
IAE	Integral Absolute Error
ISE	Integral Squared Error
ITAE	Integral Time-weighted Absolute Error
MPC	Model Predictive Control
NaOH	Sodium Hydroxide
NTU	Nephelometric Turbidity Unit
OD	Optical Density
PID	Proportional-Integral-Derivative
PUF	Poly Urathine Foam
PWM	Pulse Width Modulation
SA	Sodium Alginate
Tf	transfer function

CHAPTER 1

INTRODUCTION

1.1 INTRODUCTION

Water is major natural resource used for many domestic and industrial tasks. Water resources cover approximately 70-75% of Earth's surface. However, 7only 2.5% is freshwater suitable for human consumption. Only 0.5% is available as groundwater and 0.01% as surface water in lakes, streams, and rivers that can be easily accessed. This small volume of water is used for many purposes such as drinking, transportation, heating and cooling, industry, etc., by the human population. In India, water scarcity problems are because of rapid population growth, lack of water treatment facilities, and lack of investment funds. At present, only about 10% of the wastewater is treated, and the rest is discharged into water bodies with no proper treatment, which consequently pollute water bodies. Recycling the wastewater in an effective manner to fulfill the increasing water demand and protect the health of water bodies is an essential requirement.

1.2 SIGNIFICANCE OF THE RESEARCH

The wastewater treatment process is one of the chemical processes that satisfy the human community's basic necessity. It is necessary to supply high-quality drinking water. The traditional wastewater treatment plant consists of the primary and secondary clarifier.

In these modern times, the industrial implementation of advanced control techniques for the process industries has become more demanding, mainly because of the increasing complexity of the processes and enhanced requirements in product quality and environmental factors. Therefore, the process industries need more reliable, accurate, efficient, and flexible control systems for the process plant's operation. To fulfill the requirements, there is a continuing need for research on improved forms of control. Control of industrial processes is difficult because several reasons due to their nonlinear dynamic behavior, uncertain and time-varying parameters, constraints in a manipulated variable, the interaction between manipulated and controlled variables, unmeasured and frequent disturbances dead time input, and measurements.

1.3 NEED FOR THE RESEARCH

The current economic and environmental concerns require an approach for increasing productivity, enhancing the quality of the product, reducing downtime and operating costs with the sole objective to optimize the use of resources (raw material, power, labor/human resources, etc.) and process efficiency. It can be achieved by automation, which introduces scientific techniques to automate the system's operation and control to decrease human intervention and improve the system's productivity and efficiency.

Manual operation control consists of a collection of physical samples and their testing in a standard laboratory. Accordingly, the control elements are changed manually to maintain the water quality parameters within the desired ranges. As the technology becomes affordable direct measurement instrument like online sensors, portable spectrophotometers, and handheld meters has replaced the standard laboratory testing methods. Even though affordable optimization has not been done due to the time lag between measurements and control elements adjustment.

The wastewater treatment is important to protect and maintain the health of the rivers/lakes failing. The water bodies' health is under deterioration, thereby threatening public health, wildlife habitat, fisheries, recreation, and ultimately human lives quality. The treated wastewater can also be used for purposes where drinking water quality is not needed.

1.4 CURRENT STATUS OF POLLUTION DUE TO TEXTILE INDUSTRIES

A textile unit has both dry and wet processing of raw materials. The textile manufacturing process is characterized by the large consumption of resources like water, fuel, and a wide range of chemicals in an improved process sequence that results in a significant amount of waste. Textile processing units generate a huge quantity of solid and liquid waste, and some may be hazardous. The nature of the waste produced depends on the type of fibers, chemical substances involved in the textile process, the methods and technologies adopted for processing. The major environmental problems linked with textile manufacturing are typically those associated with water body pollution caused by raw effluents' discharge. Dyeing and finishing units contribute a key share in wastewater generation which uses a high amount of water throughout its process, starting from the washing of fibers, bleaching, dyeing, and washing of refined products. About two hundred liters of water is required to make one kilogram of textile product. This large amount of wastewater is generated as a mixture of compounds from all wet and dry processes. It can cause harm to society if proper treatment is not taken before being discharged into the environment. Wet processing such as dyeing and bleaching in textile manufacturing utilizes color removal liquids (peroxide), beverage powder, caustic soda, sulphuric acid, sodium peroxide, hydrochloric acid, dyes, and chemicals. Also, other unfounded chemicals contain a range of dyes or heavy metals, which are carcinogenic. Mainly these chemicals are not preserved in the finished hosiery supplies, however, released as wastewater.

1.5 STAGES OF WASTEWATER TREATMENT PROCESS

The three types of wastewater treatment facilities are sewage treatment plants, effluent treatment plants, and common effluent treatment plants. These plants treat wastewater to make it more compatible or acceptable for human consumption or discharge into a water body. This review focuses solely on a common effluent treatment facility that treats effluents from small and medium-sized industrial units. Specific treatment of the wastewater from individual industrial units may have a considerable concentration of contaminants, making it techno-economically impracticable to reduce them to the necessary concentration. Furthermore, the common effluent treatment plant offers a more cost-effective and efficient choice for neutralization.

To protect and sustain the health of the rivers/lakes failing, wastewater treatment is required. The health of the water bodies is deteriorating, posing a threat to public health, wildlife habitat, recreational fishing, and, ultimately, the quality of human life. The treated wastewater can also be used for other uses that do not necessitate drinking water purity.

Sravanthi Animireddy (2015) has discussed the different stages of the wastewater treatment process. The various stages have been described in the subsections.

1.5.1 Physicochemical treatment

The wastewater collected in the collecting sump is pumped to the physicochemical treatment section using a raw effluent transfer pump in the physicochemical treatment section. In a flash mixer, the effluent is treated with a lime solution and ferrous alum to elevate the pH to 8. The effluent is transferred to the flocculation stage, where ferric alum is added once more to carry out flocculation and coagulation of suspended and precipitated particles as they pass through the reaction channel, where a suitable polyelectrolyte is added to increase the coagulated and flocculated mass's settling rate.

1.5.2 Primary Clarifier

The coagulation process is a fast mixing process. The coagulation process removes the suspended solids present in the water. Alum is used as a coagulant in this process. Samadi et al. (2010) and Lee et al. (2012) have discussed various coagulants in the leachate treatment process. The alternate coagulants that may be used are as follows:

- Sodium aluminate
- Ferric sulfate
- Ferrous sulfate
- Ferric chloride
- Polymers

The coagulation process is a chemical process where the coagulant neutralizes suspended solids' charge and thereby forms a sticky substance called "flocs." The salts of iron or aluminum are used as coagulants in this stage. The reaction between the water and any one of the above coagulants produces "flocs." The formation of "flocs" is an important characteristic of the coagulation process.

1.5.3 Flocculation

Flocculation is a slow mixing process. The slow mixing increases the probability of collision between the flocs formed during the coagulation process. Because of the sticky nature of flocs, the smaller size flocs stick together and forms larger flocs. The main purpose of this process is to increase the size of flocs to be removed easily in the next stage.

1.5.4 Sedimentation

In the sedimentation process treated water from the flocculation, the stage is allowed to flow very slowly. The detention time of this stage is higher than the previous stages. The bigger-sized flocs from the previous stage begin to settle at the bottom of the sedimentation basin due to gravity. The flocs settled at the bottom of the sedimentation basin are called sludge. The sludge is removed periodically from the sedimentation basin.

1.5.5 Filtration

The suspended solids present in the raw water are removed by coagulation, flocculation, and sedimentation processes. The smaller size particles may be removed using the filtration process. The filter is made up of layers of sand, charcoal, and gravel. The water from the sedimentation process is allowed to pass through the filter to remove the smaller particles. The filtration process removes suspended particles, manganese precipitates, smaller size flocs, microorganisms, iron, and silt.

1.5.6 Disinfection

Disinfection is another important stage in the water treatment process. This process ensures the elimination of bacteria and other harmful algae from drinking water. To reduce tooth decay, fluoride is added to the water. Worldwide public health groups have recommended the fluoridation process. It is an effective and economical process. Fluoride is used as either a dry powder or a solution. This disinfection process destroys or disables the disease-causing organisms. Another commonly used disinfectant is chlorine because of its effectiveness in destroying disease-causing organisms. Chlorine dissolves rapidly in the water. Care should be taken that only the required amount of chlorine is added to the water. Normally the disinfection process is carried out in the distribution stage of the water treatment plant.

Table 1.1 Physicochemical Characteristics of Dyeing Waste Water

Characteristics	Scouring	Bleaching	Mercerising	Dye-Ing	Composite	BIS Discharge limit (inland water)
Color	-	-	High Color	Strong Color	Strong Color	Colorless
pH	10-12	8.5-11	8-10	9-11	8-10	5.6 - 9.0
TDS (mg/l)	12,000-30,000	2500-11,000	2000-2600	1500-4000	5000-10,000	2100

Table 1.1 (Continued)

TSS (mg/l)	1000-2000	200-400	100-400	50-350	100-700	100
BOD (mg/l)	2500-3500	100-500	50-120	100-400	50-550	30
COD (mg/l)	10,000-20,000	1200-1600	250-400	400-1400	250-8000	250
Chlorides - (mg/l)			350-700	-	100-500	1000
Sulphates - (mg/l)			100-350	-	50-300	1000

Table 1.1 shows the Physicochemical Characteristics of Dyeing Waste Water, Khandegar V et al., (2013)

1.5.7 Storage and Distribution

Water storage is a common process that is similar to the water stored in houses. Water is stored in a closed tank or reservoir to protect from disease-causing organisms and other pollutants. The treated water is stored to meet the demands of the communities. Then the water is distributed to the human community through the pipelines.

1.6 EFFECT OF DYES ON HUMAN AND ECOSYSTEMS

Dyes are harmful when consumed or inhaled and are classified as an obnoxious category of pollutants that cause skin irritation and can cause cancer. These are also quite unappealing from an aesthetic standpoint. They take a long time to biodegrade and may be toxic to plants and animals. Because color in water bodies blocks the flow of sunlight, it has an impact on aquatic variety.

1.7 BASIC CONCEPTS OF THE PRESENT STUDY

Supplying good quality drinking water throughout the year is a major issue faced by the human community. During rain or floods, the water quality is highly affected by the suspended particles. The traditional treatment methods may not be able to supply good quality drinking water. This research proposes a solution to supply good quality drinking water throughout the year. Another issue related to water faced by the present generation is water scarcity. In many places survival of people is affected by water scarcity. At the same time, water is wasted in many ways. During rainfall, water flows over the ground, gets mixed with mud and dirt, and becomes unsuitable for drinking. The rainwater may also get collected in ponds and lakes. The water in ponds and lakes may get polluted with suspended solids making the water unsuitable for drinking. These suspended solids increase the turbidity of water. The current study aims at providing a solution for the above problems.

The conventional water treatment plant contains three main processes, namely coagulation, flocculation, and sedimentation. The same processes have been proposed at a small-scale level for laboratory purposes. This helps in implementing various types of control algorithms to treat the water with high efficiency. The control algorithm used to decide the chemical dosage to be added in the water treatment process's coagulation stage and thereby reduce the turbidity of the water. This ensure the supply of good quality drinking water throughout the year. The control algorithm and the prototype that has been developed can be used in any type of raw water treatment and thereby reduce water scarcity. This will guarantee the supply of a sufficient amount of good quality drinking water to the human community throughout the year.

1.8 OBJECTIVES OF THE STUDY

The following are the objective of the thesis.

- To analyze the parameters of textile effluents.
- To design a controller for removal of color, Neutralization of pH, and reduction of dissolved oxygen concentration from wastewater.
- To find the potency of treat water by analyzing them with the present study.

1.9 SCOPE OF THE PRESENT STUDY

This study focuses on the color removal of textile industry wastewater in the Tirupur region using Poly Urathene Foam and Salinium Alginate methods which address the need for techno-economically feasible options in treating the effluent. The proposed pH neutralization and DO control method replicates the feedback control strategy. The prototype developed in this research may be used as a portable Wastewater treatment.

1.10 AIM AND SCOPE OF THE RESEARCH

This thesis consists of seven chapters. Chapter 1 defines the necessity of wastewater treatment process. The aim and scope of this study are declared. The techniques used in water treatment are mentioned in this section of the work is explained chapter wise.

Many research papers and books were referred for this research work, and a few of them have been described briefly in chapter 2. The controller techniques were applied based on the literature on pH, dissolved oxygen, and color removal.

The bio-process setup was made to remove the Color in chapter 3. PID controller was designed to automate this process. The dye solution was prepared, and the Color was measured using a color sensor that has four channels.

Chapter 4 includes the experimental methods and the experiment's observations, which are required to develop a controller algorithm. The real-time pH neutralization process has been implemented and discussed in this chapter.

The development of dissolved oxygen control using PID is described in chapter 5.

Chapter 6 summarizes and represents the whole work and Few future enhancements have been suggested in this chapter.

CHAPTER 2

LITERATURE SURVEY

A detailed literature survey was done covering the topic of pH, Dissolved Oxygen, and color removal. Around 120 articles have been surveyed and few are listed here. The summary of the study is presented below, describing the objective and methodology discussed in different papers.

2.1 LITERATURE SURVEY ON pH

Pravin and Glan (Pravin & Glan, 2019) proposed the pH neutralization method using the Adaptive Neuro-Fuzzy Inference System (ANFIS). ANFIS with a hybrid set of rules is used in this paper to enhance the prediction. This paper deals with the methodology to reduce settling time, disturbance, and errors.

Estofanero et al., (Estofanero et al., 2019) demonstrates a predictive controller's experimental results implemented to a pH neutralization plant. Initial tests were carried out to get an estimated transfer function to tune a PI controller. The procedure was then realized in a closed-loop with the PI controller to acquire linear models, and the finest models were selected to implement the predictive controller.

Zanila and Hussain (Zanila & Hussain, 2015) For a pH neutralization process, the author offers a multivariable fuzzy logic controller with a Lyapunov adaptive control method. Nonlinear dynamics and multi-delayed effects on input variables are observed in the minimal neutralization process condition in this study. The Takagi-Sugeno fuzzy inference system is used in the controller, which is optimized by a genetic algorithm to reduce closed-loop error. In all of the scenarios that were examined, the adaptive fuzzy controller outperformed the traditional PID controller.

Upadhye et al., (Upadhye et al., 2015) In this paper, contrasting solution is added to acid or base to attain a solution with a pH value of 7. Nonlinear control systems such as fuzzy logic and neural network-based controllers give satisfactory control performance when compared to traditional control techniques. Traditional PI controllers are incapable of satisfactorily controlling a nonlinear system. In comparison to the traditional PI controller, fuzzy logic control offers a better option. This paper provides better outputs using Fuzzy logic control for the purpose of pH neutralization process.

Hermansson and Syafiie (Hermansson & Syafiie, 2015) illustrates the various Model Predictive Control (MPC) techniques for the pH process. A full overview of the pH system and the difficulties associated in managing it is offered, followed by a broad discussion of MPC's structure. In this study, the many modelling strategies applied to the MPC, which is used to characterize the pH range, are reviewed, ranging from simple linear models to multiple linear models such as piecewise linear descriptions and fuzzy models, to nonlinear descriptions such as Wiener models.

Xiao et al., (Xiao et al., 2014) proposed for the pH neutralization process, Takagi–Sugeno fuzzy recurrent neural network (T–S FRNN) was developed. For the T–S FRNN model, there are two opposing criteria, and a

DNA-based NSGA-II is presented to optimize the model's parameters. The model optimized by DNA-based NSGA-II is more accurate, and the network's complexity is acceptable, according to the comparison results.

Pawlowskia et al., (Pawlowskia et al., 2014) proposed a method to manage the pH in a microalgae production process, an event-based model predictive control system. A sensor dead-band technique is used in conjunction with a Generalized Predictive Control (GPC) algorithm. The frequency of controller execution is modified in this method to match the dynamics of the process.

Davood et al., (Davood et al., 2013) suggested a fuzzy control strategy for the pH neutralization process using the Wiener model. One of the advantages of this control structure is that it takes explicit constraints into account when controlling systems that are part of the proposed fuzzy predictive control. Finally, the proposed approach is tested using a pH neutralization process model.

Abdullah et al., (Abdullah et al., 2012) proposed the pH neutralization procedure, which is widely used in wastewater treatment and process industries such as biotechnology, chemical processing, and pharmaceuticals. Because of the very nonlinear nature of the process, controlling pH neutralization is recognized to be a difficult task.

Javier et al., (Javier et al., 2012) report the design and implementation of an innovative automated chlorination system at the Sant Joan Despi drinking water treatment plant (Barcelona, Spain). Two problems arose: first, the influence of dead time inherent in the measurement of process variables of water and their dose was decreased; and second, the system was equipped with the ability to adjust to changes in water quality and the presence of ammonium in the treated water. The obtained results of a feed forward control method in combination with a basic feedback mechanism are satisfactory.

Jorgensen et al., (Jorgensen et al., 2012) proposed a bioreactor in combination with an electrically powered membrane separation process as a potential technique for enhancing lactic acid bioproduction. To govern the dynamic system, a plan for control structure design is proposed. The theoretical design of the control structure is based on a sensitivity analysis. The sensitivity index is calculated using dynamic simulations. A periodic input-resetting control structure is chosen based on the analysis. The system uses the imposed current density to adjust pH and resets the current density to regulate the dialysate channel's hydroxide intake concentration. The control structure in REED regularly obtains the desired pH at the feed channel output and resets the current density. As a result, adequate performance can be achieved over a considerable portion of the operating window.

Andre et al., (Andre et al., 2011) presents a fuzzy controller for pH neutralization using the Mamdani model. This controller was applied for the pH alteration in different kinds of waters like soap, rainwaters, etc. and hence making it reusable for other domestic purposes. These simulations are done in a MATLAB® Simulink platform and established in PIC 18F4550, representing the aids of the fuzzy logic’s application in this method.

Hermansson et al., (Hermansson et al., 2010) illustrates the control approach that utilizes a piecewise linear depiction of the process. The linear model is applied in an MPC to establish an optimal control. The process performance was studied by applying it for a pH neutralization setup which establishes a better tracking of setpoint deviations and rapid reduction of fluctuations.

Shahin et al., (Shahin et al., 2009) discuss an adaptive control strategy established on fuzzy logic systems for pH control is described. For the implementation of the suggested scheme, no composition measurement is needed. The stability of the closed-loop system is established. The result of the closed-loop system appears to be homogeneously eventually bounded, and asymptotical stability is achieved under specific conditions. Simulation and experimental investigations are used to evaluate the proposed controller's effectiveness. The suggested controller outperforms a tuned PI controller in terms of set-point tracking and load rejection, according to the results.

Alwan (Alwan, 2008) proposed experimental research on pH-control challenges of industrial electroplating wastewater treatment plants. Most issues and interruptions in the normal operation of the water treatment may be solved with the accurate and sensitive PID control system. However, traditional treatment was phased out in favour of a proprietary treatment agent known as a QUASIL, which was more effective across a wider pH range.

Mohamed et al., (Mohamed et al., 2008) examined pH behavior because of the logarithmic link between hydrogen ions concentrations [H+] and pH level. The viability of the mathematical model that depicts the process is critical to the development of the control mechanism. This research compares the performance of an artificial neural network predictive controller to that of more typical PID controllers and shows that empirical modelling of the pH neutralization plant is possible. Finally, a workable empirical model that is closest to a second-order with dead time has been discovered. Artificial neural network predictive controllers outperformed traditional PI / PID controllers.

Ayla (Ayla, 2007) proposed the design and development of a Generalized Predictive Control (GPC) employed to a pH neutralization process. The control objective is to control the optimal pH value at the desired set point irrespective of the variations in feed flow rate. The ARIMAX model related to pH and flow rate was developed. The model parameters were developed using Bierman and Genetic algorithms.

Syafiie et al., (Syafiie et al., 2007) suggests the design of model-free learning control for the pH neutralization process. The MFLC is preferred due to the severe nonlinear and time-varying behavior of the system. This algorithm can also be applied to systems whose model cannot be developed. Results obtained using this algorithm were compared with the conventional PI algorithm.

Kostas et al., (Kostas et al., 2006) This paper discusses remote monitoring and control of pH via IDAC-1 board. The computer is made as to the server, and the IDAC-1 board is the client. Client-server model communications have been configured for remote monitoring and control of pH via the Internet.

Bernt et al., (Bernt et al., 2005) proposed model predictive control of nonlinear sampled-data systems focusing on computational efficiency. The quasi-linear models have been developed for the systems and model predictive control to implement the closed-loop control. To reduce the online computational burden, neural network approximates were used to approximate the optimal model.

Audun and Sigurd (Audun & Sigurd, 2004) Control-related difficulties for the neutralization process are discussed in this study. The neutralization is usually done in several steps (mixing tanks) with a modest decrease in concentration, primarily for control reasons. It was suggested that identical tanks with total volume Vtot be utilized with local PI or PID control in each tank, where Vtot is a function of kd, the time delay in each tank, the flow rate q, and the number of tanks n. This gives Vtot = 2qnk1/n d for kd 1, which is usual in pH-neutralization.

Gomez et al., (Gomez et al., 2004) suggest Wiener model identification and predictive control of a pH neutralization process in this paper. The wiener model identified is used as the internal model in a predictive model controller. This MPC is used to control the white box simulation model. The performance of the WMPC was matched with that of a linear Model Predictive Controller and with more traditional feedback control, i.e., a Proportional Integral Derivative control. Simulation results express the WMPC overtakes the LMPC and the PID controllers.

Nio et al., (Nio et al., 2002) designed a Fuzzy based PID Controller for pH neutralization plants. A Simulink tool kit of MATLAB was used to develop the process model based on the McAvoy model. The gain scheduling of K_P in the PID controller was developed using a fuzzy control algorithm. The Fuzzy PI controller was then put to the test on servo and regulator issues. A uniform random number generator was used in the servo test to replicate set points between pH=3 and pH=11, and the simulation was conducted for 100s. The regulator test was carried out at a rate of 55% acid flow, Fa. The servo test yielded a nearly perfect response, with no overshoot or oscillator reactions. The controller's performance was found to be good, with a very quick response time and nearly no lag time. The regulator test resulted in a response that fluctuated in response to the shocks but was limited to a pH range of 0.01 pH units.

Kyu et al., (Kyu et al., 1999) propose to regulate the pH process, focus on developing a new fuzzy-model-based predictive control system. The control strategy is based on a fuzzy Takagi-Sugeno model of the regulated process. The process model retains a linear representation of fuzzy roles' conclusion sections in the current fuzzy model predictive control approach. As a result, it has a substantial advantage over other types of models in that it can successfully manage nonlinear processes by embedding the linear characteristic. The predictive control technique was built using a fuzzy model of the pH process to be regulated. The efficiency of the current control system was shown by computer simulations and experiments.

Flemming and Mogens (Flemming & Mogens, 1979) the pH-neutralization process is controlled by a self-tuning regulator. Due to large fluctuations in process sensitivity with pH and process nonlinearities, the process is difficult to manage. Even though the process is nonlinear, experiments on a pilot plant show that a self-tuning pH-regulator with exponential forgetting and optimal quadratic control has adequate static and dynamic features. The self-tuning algorithm is also shown to respond to changes in process conditions, suggesting that it could be a viable alternative to standard Pl-controllers.

2.2 LITERATURE SURVEY ON DISSOLVED OXYGEN

Man et al., (Man et al., 2018) Propose two control techniques for dissolved oxygen content in the sequential batch reactor of the wastewater treatment process in the papermaking industry: neural network-based PID and fuzzy-based PID. The performance was analyzed by comparing conventional PID with neural network-based PID and Fuzzy base PID. The backpropagation algorithm is used in a neural-based controller. The results prove that the fuzzy-based PID controller outperforms the other two-controller.

Nguyen et al., (Nguyen et al., 2018) In this paper, the design methodology of the coefficients of adjustment of classical PI controller based on hedge algebras approach (HA - Hedge Algebras) to improve the quality of operation of the system has been presented. The adjustment works online with a wide range of adjustments enough around the value calculated by Ziegler-Nichols's empirical methods. Subjects selected for trial are the controller method for dissolved oxygen in the wastewater treatment system by activated sludge method. Through system simulation in Matlab or Simulink environment at some different reference values, the results have been evaluated for quality control. The response time and overshoot reduce significantly, and the static deviation level is small. These results can be tested on the control system for more complex subjects to evaluate the effectiveness of methods and practical applications on industrial control systems.

Xianjun et al., (Xianjun et al., 2018) The control of DO using a conventional PID controller is discussed in this paper. Since the PID controller is supposed to be non-adaptive, a neural network-based PID control algorithm is proposed in this paper. The neural network was trained using Radial Basis Function (RBF). The efficient learning capacity and adaptability of RBF make it more reliable with improved performance.

Mana et al., (Mana et al., 2017) This study discusses a fuzzy logic system with PID (Fuzzy-PID controller) for controlling dissolved oxygen content. The suggested paper mill wastewater treatment process is based on a sequential batch reactor simulation model of the paper mill wastewater treatment process that has been created. The criteria used in Benchmark Simulation Model No. 1 were used to investigate and assess a case study with noise. The Fuzzy-PID controller has better control indices than the standard PID controller, according to simulation findings with white noise on dissolved oxygen.

Robert and Adam (Robert & Adam, 2015) for tracking dissolved oxygen, the author suggests a fuzzy control system. In the wastewater treatment process, biological processes are complicated, multivariable, time-varying, and nonlinear. In this research, the sequencing batch reactor and aeration were modelled and verified. Inverse model development was used to model the system, and appropriate control mechanisms were used. Simulation was used to test the nonlinear fuzzy control system, which was based on real data records from a case study plant in Swarzewo, Northern Poland.

Karol et al., (Karol et al., 2014) the management of dissolved oxygen levels during the nitrification phase is discussed in this work. The aeration process, which includes blowers, pipes, diffusers, and other nonlinear elements, provides oxygen. This work proposes and develops an aeration system that is modelled after an adaptive control system with an anti-windup filter.

Yuge et al., (Yuge et al., 2014) the generalized dynamic fuzzy neural network modelling (GDFNN) method was used to estimate the change in dissolved oxygen concentration in the activated sludge wastewater treatment process. Because the width of the elliptical basis function (EBF) will be set according to the relevance of input variables, this method employs an elliptical basis function (EBF) as its fuzzy membership function. Additionally, characteristics such as self-organization, online learning, and rule trimming can improve the dissolved oxygen concentration model's accuracy and generalization capacity.

Mat and Zain (Mat & Zain, 2012) the simulation of modelling a flexible plate system, which will be employed as a new way to manufacture dissolved oxygen, is proposed in this work. In comparison to other studies in this subject, this strategy is reversed. The movement of the flexible plate will induce waves and bubbles in the water, which will generate dissolved oxygen for the tiger prawn's pond. The simulation's outcomes are presented.

Ciprian et al., (Ciprian et al., 2012) the purpose of this research is to discuss how to effectively control dissolved oxygen concentrations in wastewater treatment systems. For dissolved oxygen concentration control, the Gain Scheduling control approach was chosen. To begin, the dissolved oxygen control loop was identified experimentally at various operating points. The Gain Scheduling method was created in order for the closed-loop system's behavior to be consistent around the operating points stated. Simulation and an experimentally pilot plant were used to test the Gain Scheduling control method of the dissolved oxygen concentration in the article.

Zawadzki and Piotrowski (Zawadzki & Piotrowski, 2012) presented the wastewater treatment plant as a large-scale industrial system that is complicated, time-varying, multivariable, and nonlinear. Also, there are a lot of interactions between the components. The tracking of dissolved oxygen is one of the most difficult and basic problems in biological processes. An aeration system provides air to the aerated tanks (blowers, diffusers, pipes). It's a dynamic system with a lot of moving parts. The new dissolved oxygen tracking control approach in activated sludge processes is discussed. The Internal Model Control structure is used to examine a nonlinear fuzzy PI control system. For control system design, the inverse model of an aeration system is used. Simulation is used to assess a control strategy using real data from a case study plant.

Xuemei et al., (Xuemei et al., 2011) this research provides a dissolved oxygen prediction model. The RBF neural network's nonlinear approximation ability for dissolved oxygen in aquaculture pads has been established. The method serves as a foundation for the intelligent aquaculture environment monitoring systems that have been created. This paper also considers external environmental parameters such as temperature, acidity, and so on.

Liping and Kosta (Liping & Kosta, 2010) the wastewater treatment process in a large-scale system is described in detail, as is the energy-intensive process. The aeration step consumes roughly 50 to 70 percent of the total electric energy used in the urban wastewater treatment plan. The real aeration process control approach is usually simple and primitive. Using a more precise control mechanism, the overall operating cost of the wastewater treatment system can be significantly decreased. This paper developed a fuzzy logic control system for controlling the aeration process in an urban wastewater treatment plant. The oxygen transmission coefficient corresponding to the dissolved oxygen index can be modified to control the aeration process.

Shuhua et al., (Shuhua et al., 2010) discusses the impact of DO concentration on fish's growth and development. Real-time monitoring of DO in a fish pond has been discussed. Remote monitoring via Internet and SMS service for abnormal conditions has been developed. The SMS service via AT instructions on the CDMA platform was developed.

Amalendu et al., (Amalendu et al., 2010) In fed-batch fermentation of methionine production, a proposed decoupled adaptive controller for managing dissolved oxygen and glucose feeding simultaneously is discussed. The cellular synthesis of methionine is tightly controlled, and the process dynamics reveal a nonlinear relationship between glucose content and dissolved oxygen. The system is decoupled by the adaptive controller created utilizing a linear reference model for regulating these two variables.

Liangjin et al., (Liangjin et al., 2009) The Dissolved Oxygen model and set-point control were investigated in this paper utilising the Radial Basis Function Model of Neural Network. The goal of this paper is to manage the DO set point using evolutionary RBF-based ammonium concentration prediction. As a result, the modelling and control concept works well for the DO concentration impact.

Kazimierz et al., (Kazimierz et al., 2009) describes the hierarchical control for dissolved oxygen reference trajectory tracking in the activated sludge process. A nonlinear MPC control algorithm is discussed in this paper. Two-level control, LLC- Lower level control and High-level control-HLC, has been implemented in this process for DO Control.

Holenda et al., (Holenda et al., 2008) A novel MPC-based control algorithm is discussed in this paper. The need for control of dissolved oxygen is justified in this paper. The effect of tuning parameters like prediction horizon, input weights, and sampling time are discussed in this paper. The results were promising and effective, and Hence the use of MPC for Dissolved Oxygen control is Justified.

Han et al., (Han et al., 2008) In their paper addresses the design, application and simulation of a novel type of softly switched Takagi-Sugeno fuzzy PI control system for dissolved oxygen concentration (DO) tracking at the wastewater treatment plant (WWTP). The suggested control system is designed, including tuning the PI controllers, entirely based on the experimental data. This control system is tested by simulation.

Zhe et al., (Zhe et al., 2008) The Hammerstein model was used to offer a Nonlinear Constrained Model Predictive Control (NCMPC) method for controlling dissolved oxygen in a bioreactor system. The stirrer speed is varied as an input to control the output of dissolved oxygen. With no input limitations, the suggested controller was compared to the Nonlinear Model Predictive Control (NMPC) technique. Experiments and simulations are carried out. To carry out the studies, a control system based on the PIC16F877 microprocessor was created. The simulation and experimental results show that with input constraints, the input stirrer speed performs better than when there are no input limitations. Simulations under known disturbances and changing set-point tracking demonstrate the effectiveness of the proposed controller.

Raynitchka (Raynitchka, 2007) emphases on two common Proportional Integral Derivative controller tuning methodologies for Dissolved Oxygen control. As part of an adaptive control mechanism, this has been implemented. In Matlab/Simulink Software, procedures for real-time execution of tuning algorithms and calculated controls are implemented. The COST benchmark, the ASM1 biological model, and the University of Cape Town process structures are all used in the computations.

Matthew and Reza (Matthew & Reza, 2002) The idea of building a generic sensor model for analysis and low-level design through simulation in the wastewater treatment sector is investigated in this work. Sensor models are not required in most simulators since the measurement data is expected to be an accurate depiction of the real-time condition. Sensor readings in the hostile wastewater environment are prone to corruption and errors, thus understanding their behavior is critical for low-level control applications. As a result, sensor validation processes are critical for maintaining a stable closed-loop system. A brief discussion of PCA for inspecting sensor failures is presented, as well as an example of how the general sensor model can be utilized to construct a dissolved oxygen (DO) sensor model. There's also a comparison with a physical sensor.

Vincent et al., (Vincent et al., 1998) have presented a detailed report on dissolved oxygen's fuzzy control. Also, the fuzzy control strategy is compared with the PID self-tuning method of control for wastewater treatment.

Insufficient DO concentration degrades the water quality and makes aquatic life difficult. The setpoint is optimized using an objective function, including water quality and financial cost.

2.3 LITERATURE SURVEY ON COLOR REMOVAL

Hua et al., (Hua et al., 2019) discusses two-stage wastewater reuse treatment to improve water quality and reuse water. The initial treatment process incorporated a flocculation and sedimentation system with two sand filtration units, oxidation unit, ultrafiltration, and Reverse osmosis (RO) system. The second system has an ozonation unit, a sand filtration unit, UF and RO system. This combined process enhanced the performance of the system.

Wioletta et al., (Wioletta et al., 2018), in their paper, describes the decolorization of wastewater containing dyes. This paper focuses on decolorizing two specific types of dyes belonging to two different types of classes. The solid support implanted absorbed dyes at a negligible level. The results proved better for strains BWPH & RWP17. The efficiency was increased in samples with dead fungus biomass.

Yingying et al., (Yingying et al., 2017) The biodegradation of colors in anaerobic, aerobic, anaerobic-aerobic, and anaerobic-aerobic settings, as well as dye degradation by microorganisms, are discussed in this work. China's total dye production is estimated to be around 900,000 tonnes. Dyes are utilized in a variety of sectors, including textiles, foods, papermaking, and plastics. A huge amount of dye wastewater is produced in these businesses, and dye contamination alters the watercolor, improves eutrophication, reduces oxygen, and, as a result, greatly disturbs aquatic species. Dye wastewater has become a major source of pollution. Dye biodegradation has received a lot of attention in recent years.

Merih and Mine (Merih & Mine, 2017) screened 40 fungi for their ability to decolorize Xiron orange RHD (FW), Tobactive scarlet P2R, and Xiron orange RHD (FW) in their paper (Kimsa). Microorganisms with the ability to decolorize organic colorants were isolated from the Porsuk stream, soil, and wastewater at the textile industry. This research used four Fusarium, Penicillium expansum, P. citreo-viride, Aspergillus flavipes, Trichoderma harzianum, and Paecilomyes variotii strains. In addition to these strains, different Myrothecium strains were employed in this investigation. Maximum decolorization was observed at 25oC pH 7.0 utilising those strains. A. flavipes had the most decolorization of all of them. T. harzianum was next, followed by Fusarium SP2 and T. harzianum. The B.O.D. of these strains has dropped. Textile manufacturing effluent had 17.7% and 24.2 percent concentrations, respectively.

Barathi and Indra (Barathi & Indra, 2015) In their paper focuses on the significance of Azo dyes. Azo dyes are significant because it is used in major industries like textile, paper, food, leather, cosmetics, and pharmaceutical industries. These wastewaters are treated with various Physio-chemical methods for treating textile effluent. Hence bio-degradation techniques are supposed to be eco-friendly without hazards.

Lavanya et al., (Lavanya et al., 2014) Describes the importance of mining dyes in industry and the effective ways of removing them. Recalcitrant Azo dyes cannot be removed from effluents and biodegradation by the aerobic and anaerobic process. The factors affecting temperature, dye concentration, decolorization are pH, effects of carbon dioxide and nitrogen, agitation, dye structure, electron donor, and enzymes involved in microbial decolorization of dyes also been high lightened in the review.

Amir and Gevorg (Amir & Gevorg, 2014) have explored how biological treatments compare in terms of turbidity and color reduction. When compared to traditional biological treatment systems in pulp mills, this treatment method achieves a significant reduction in color and turbidity.

Malgorzata and Kutylowska (Malgorzata & Kutylowska, 2011) proposed an ANN-based model to evaluate water quality after coagulation and ultrafiltration processes using an immersed membrane; various structures of multilayer perceptron with one hidden layer were created. Feedwater turbidity, turbidity in a tank, pH and temperature in the tank, and transmembrane pressure, and permeate flux were treated as input signals.

Song et al., (Song et al., 2008) investigate the efficiency of the ozone-enhanced electrocoagulation (EC) process in the decolorization of C.I. Reactive Blue 19 in water using iron electrodes. In the EC process, the pH of the solution is crucial. It affects the solution's conductivity, hydroxide speciation, and colloidal particle zeta potential.

Mouedhen et al., (Mouedhen et al., 2008) reported that when pH was less than 3, the rate of aluminum release during electrolysis with a constant charge per volume was lower than when pH was greater than 3. The effects of various operating parameters such as initial pH, initial dye concentration, current density, salt concentration, temperature, ozone flow rate, and distance between electrodes on decolorization efficiency in a laboratory-scale reactor were determined. The other operating factors had both positive and negative effects.

Daneshvar et al., (Daneshvar et al., 2005) propose that the color removal efficiency with Fe and Al electrodes is maximum when the dye solution's pH is between 5.5 and 8.5. The results of these analyses showed that the final outlet stream from the photoreactor was completely mineralized.

Pavanelli and Bigi (Pavanelli & Bigi, 2005) have presented the normal procedure to find suspended sediment concentration was the gravimetric method. This method was a direct measure of suspended sediment concentration in a water sample. The authors used Imhoff cones as an alternative indirect method for measuring suspended sediment concentration. From the analysis, it was understood that there is a close relationship between turbidity and suspended sediment concentration.

CHAPTER 3

PROCESS OPTIMIZATION OF COLOR REMOVAL

3.1 INTRODUCTION

Even in small quantities, dye materials greatly influence the visibility, appearance, and quality of water which is esthetically unpleasant. So it should be recycled without contamination. A general method, i.e., contact type color intensity measurements, leads to contamination of dye chemicals, and it is very difficult to choose the materials to avoid contamination. The optical method of measurement would be suitable for measuring color without contamination as it is a non-contact type.

In all the compounds, the reason for Color is Azo-bond (N=N), as shown in Figure 3.1. The concentration depends in the compounds depends on the strength of the double bond.

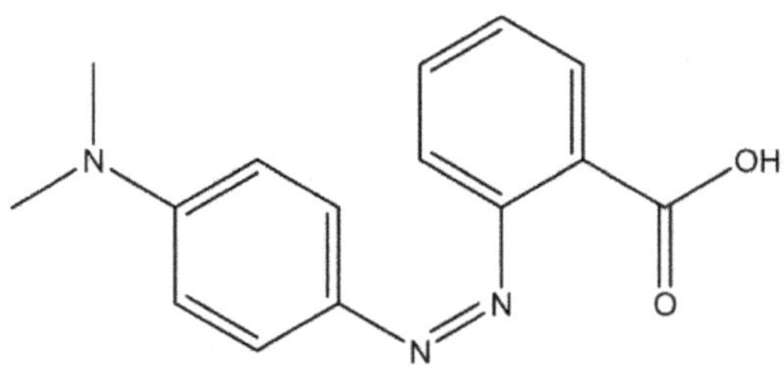

Figure 3.1 Azo Bond Structure in Color Compounds

The whole color removal process is implemented in two steps. The first steps involve measurement of color concentration using color sensor TCS3200, and the second step involves the removal of Color using Poly

Urathine Foam (PUF) and Sodium Alginate (SA). The whole setup was operated in a feedback plus feed-forward loop with an optimal control algorithm implemented in LabVIEW. The PUF (Poly Urethane Foam) is attained after the preparation process is filled together to form a filter. In the experimental setup, 12 pieces of 1*1*1 PUF are filled together to treat dye solution. The alginate beads are bound together to form a filter bed.

To calibrate the color sensor TCS3200, the spectrophotometer is used here that measure the color concentration in terms of optical density. Various known color concentrated samples were prepared and measured using color sensor TCS3200 & spectrophotometer. Among the four filter modes available in the color sensor, the blue filter was chosen for the experiment as it shows much variation for each concentration.

3. 2. PREPARATION PROCEDURE OF SOLUTION AND BIO-FILTER

3.2.1 Encapsulation of Bacteria in Alginate Beads

The experimental bacterial strain was isolated from effluent sludge of the textile industry. The organism was immobilized in alginate beads. For this process, bacterial cells developed overnight in culture media and harvested at 7000 rpm for 10 minutes. The cells were washed with 0.9% NaCl solution and suspended in sodium alginate (2.0% w/v). This slurry was then extruded drop-wise into Calcium chloride (4.0% w/v) solution. $CaCl_2$ acts as a cross-linking agent which stabilizes the beads. They were left undisturbed in the $CaCl_2$ solution for 10-12 hours, after which excessive cells were washed off with saline. The diameter of the beads was in the range of 2mm to 5mm. The whole procedure was done under aseptic conditions. The beads with the bacteria were then used for decolorization experiments.

The efficient bacterial strain (Aneurinibacillus aneurinilyticus), which effectively decolorized the selected textile dye, was immobilized in calcium alginate beads. For immobilization, the bacterial cells were grown overnight, harvested by centrifugation at 7000 rpm for ten minutes, and the pellet washed with saline and was suspended in sodium alginate. The cells-alginate mixture was dripped into $CaCl_2$ solution, which is a cross-linking agent to form calcium alginate beads. Beads were allowed to harden in calcium chloride solution for 10-12 hrs at 4°C and were then washed with saline to remove the excess of $CaCl_2$ and free cells. The diameter of beads was found to be in the range of 2 mm to 5 mm. The calcium alginate beads with immobilized cells were then used for decolorization study. The whole procedure of immobilization was carried out under aseptic conditions. Figure 3.2 shows the preparation of biofilter Sodium Alginate.

Figure 3.2 SA (Sodium Alginate) Preparation

3.2.2 Immobilization of iron nanoparticles on the polymer substrate

Polymers of unlike pore sizes were obtained from a vendor and were cut into uniform sizes. The polymer was pretreated by soaking them in a dilute HCl solution (4% v/v) over 9 – 13 hours. Entirely the mandatory reagents required for nanoparticle synthesis viz., 1.0 M Ferric chloride ($FeCl_3$), 1.6 M Sodium borohydride ($NaBH_4$), and 0.1% Palladium acetate [$Pd(CH_3COO)_2$]

were prepared using 40% ethanol. Iron nanoparticles were then synthesized onto the matrices by the sodium borohydride reduction method. Palladium acetate was doped onto the synthesized nanoparticles to enhance the activity.

Carrier matrices of different pore sizes were purchased from a local supplier (pink, yellow, white, orange). They were cut into uniform sizes of 1x1x1 cm. A dilute hydrochloric acid solution (4%) was prepared, and the cubes were soaked into it for 8 – 12 hours. All the required reagents were prepared using 40% ethanol (1.0 M Ferric chloride, 1.6 M Sodium borohydride, 0.1% Palladium acetate). The pre-treated matrices were dipped in ferric chloride solution followed by sodium borohydride solution, resulting in the formation of nanoparticles over the matrix. They were then transferred into palladium acetate to improvise the activity of the nanoparticles. These cubes were then used for the decolorization experiments. Figure 3.3 shows the preparation of Poly Urethene Foam.

Figure 3.3 PUF (Poly Urethane Foam) Preparation

3.2.3 Sample Dye Preparation

Sample dye (Red-RR) was collected from the textile industry, and its predefined concentration should mix it. The dye collected is RED-RR, and its concentration is in water should be 100ppm (parts per million). So the dye of 20mg should be mixed with 1liter of distilled water. Likewise, different red, blue samples are collected, and according to industrial standards, they formed as a dye by treating with chemicals. Figure 3.4 shows the preparation procedure of dye sample solution.

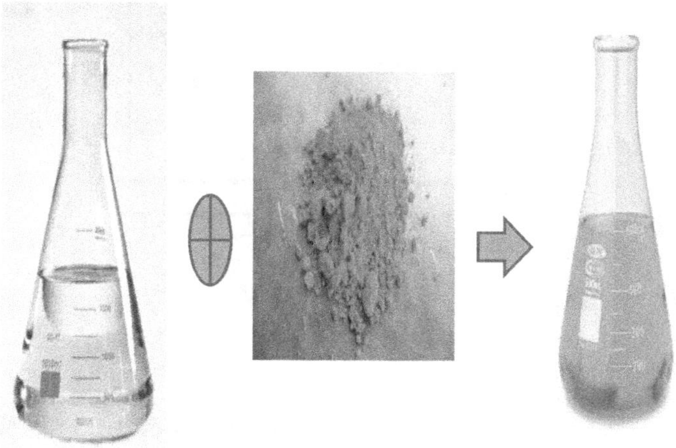

Distilled water (1lit) RED-RR Dye solution

Figure 3.4 Preparation procedure of Sample Solution

3. 3 MEASUREMENT OF COLOR

3.3.1 Color sensor

The color sensor utilized in the proposed work is an IC - TCS3200. This IC consists of an 8 x 8 array with a total of 64 photodiodes which the light-to-frequency. Out of these 64 photodiodes, 16 are used as blue(B) filter mode, another 16 photodiodes are used as green(G) filter mode, next 16 photodiodes are deployed as red(R) filter mode, and the remaining 16 photodiodes are used as white / no filter mode. The terminal S3 & S2 are used to fix the particular filter mode as per the tabulation made in Table 3. 1. To diminish the effect of variation in incident irradiance, the four filter modes are combined. Figure 3.5 shows the functional block diagram of color sensor TCS3200.

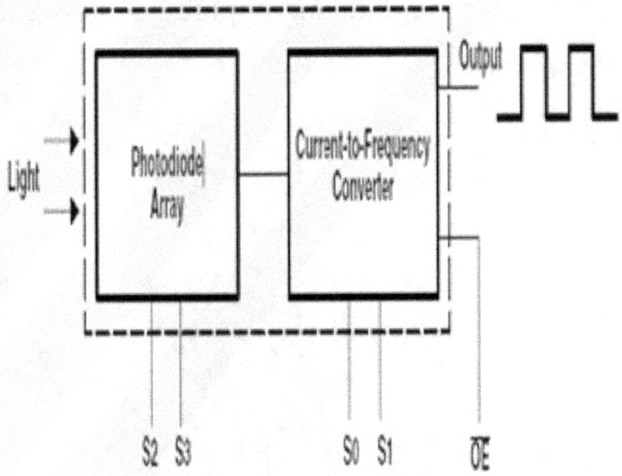

Figure 3.5 Functional Block of TCS3200

The pins S0 and S1 are used to select the scaling factor for frequency scaling as per the tabulation made in Table 3.2. By selecting the switches S0 and S1 value high, 100% scaling can be achieved. For further reducing the scaling to 20% and 2%, the switches values can be 1 0 and 0 1, respectively.

Table 3.1 Photodiode Modes

S_2	S_3	PHOTODIODE TYPES
0	0	R FILTER MODE
0	1	B FILTER MODE
1	0	No FILTER MODE
1	1	G FILTER MODE

Table 3.2 Output Frequency Scaling

S_0	S_1	FREQUENCY SCALING (fo)
0	0	Power Down
0	1	2%
1	0	20%
1	1	100%

3.3.2 Sensor Standardization

Calibration is the process of relating two unknown measurable quantities. Any sensor should be calibrated initially to meet the standards provided by the manufacture in the datasheet. The colored solutions were prepared at five different known concentrations of Red dye & Blue dye solutions and measured with TCS3200 in all the four filter modes to obtain the known solution's output frequency. And the above procedure was repeated for many solutions and tabulated. Figure 3.6 demonstrates the results of various red known concentrations for the four filter modes. Figure 3.7 displays the four filter frequency outcomes of various blue known concentrations. These grades helped in choosing the right filter mode for designing the color removal process. Table 3.3 and Table 3.4 displays the color sensor output in four different filter mode for red and blue samples respectively.

Table 3.3 Various Concentration of Red Samples

Red solution (PPM)	Red filter(KHz)	Blue filter(KHz)	Clear filter(KHz)	Green filter(KHz)
10	46.74	65.65	27.38	21.02
8	45.32	64.95	26.57	20.27
6	44.06	64.12	25.31	18.56
4	42.85	63.22	24.86	18.01
2	41.61	61.48	23.02	17.56

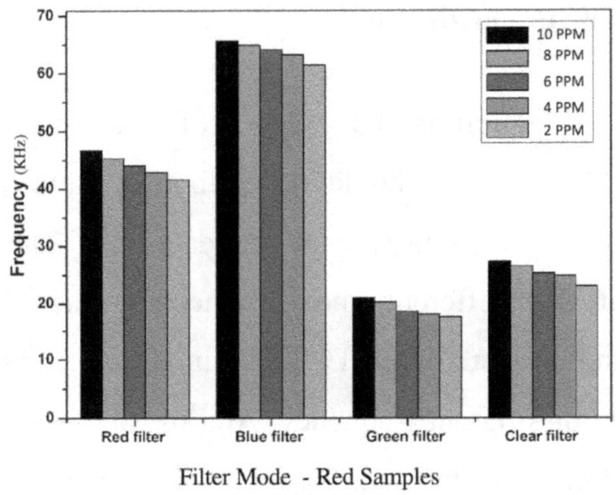

Figure 3.6 Various Concentration of Red Samples

Table 3.4 Various Concentration of Blue Samples

Blue Solution (PPM)	Red filter(KHz)	Blue filter(KHz)	Clear filter(KHz)	Green filter(KHz)
10	20.78	64.44	24.68	18.57
8	21.03	66.23	23.57	19.09
6	22.06	68.48	26.13	19.97
4	22.89	71.31	27.46	20.93
2	23.62	74.75	28.27	22.03

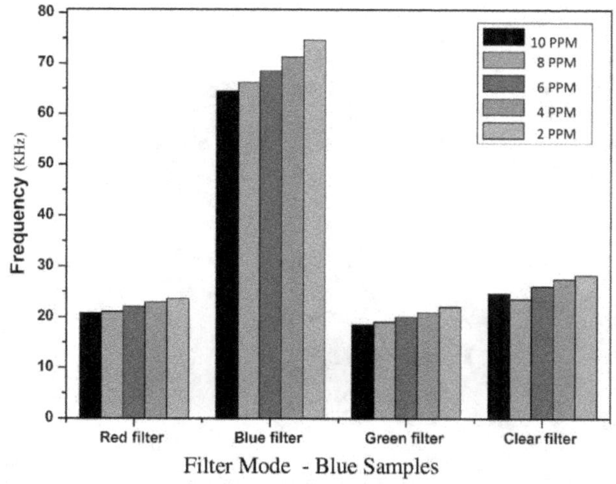

Figure 3.7 Various Concentration of Blue Samples

The calibrated color sensor is used in the bio reactor and various experiments were carried out in a batch mode to determine the de-colorization efficiency of the immobilized bacteria and immobilized nanoparticles. The same experiment was carried out in a continuous mode.

3.3.3 Color Measurement

Ten samples were prepared in each of the primary colors (Red, Green, and Blue). There are different types of photodiode used in the sensor module. According to the requirement, the channel should be chosen. To obtain a better result, it has been tested with all the available channels. To identify the concentration of each Color, optical density values are measured to calibrate the photodiode-sensor. Optical density is the degree to which refractive medium delays transmitted rays of light. Therefore each concentration, the optical value are not the same. Figure 3.8 shows the experiment setup of color measurement TCS3200.

Figure 3.8 TCS3200 Color Measurement Setup

Photodiode tuned to measure the wavelength of 640nm as per datasheet requirement, the red filter produced exact reading as per the datasheet for the dark red solution. The same can be calculated using the below formula.

$$\lambda = c / f \tag{3.1}$$

Where c = velocity of light in space ($3 * 10^8$m/s), f = frequency in Hz, λ= wavelength in nm.

Let us take a reading of 64.44 KHz (Table 3.4), then substituting the equation 3.1,

$$\lambda = (3*10^8) / (46.74*10^3) = 641.8 \text{ nm}$$

Therefore all the frequency reading output is taken at a wavelength of 640nm.

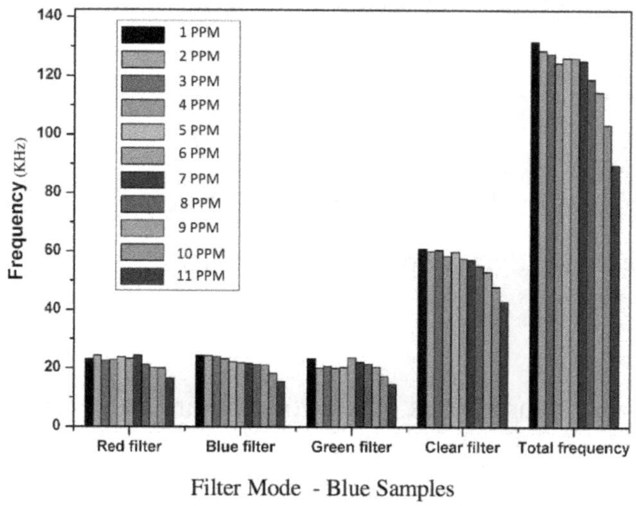

Figure 3.9 Optical Sensor Output for Various Concentrations of Blue Samples in Different Channels

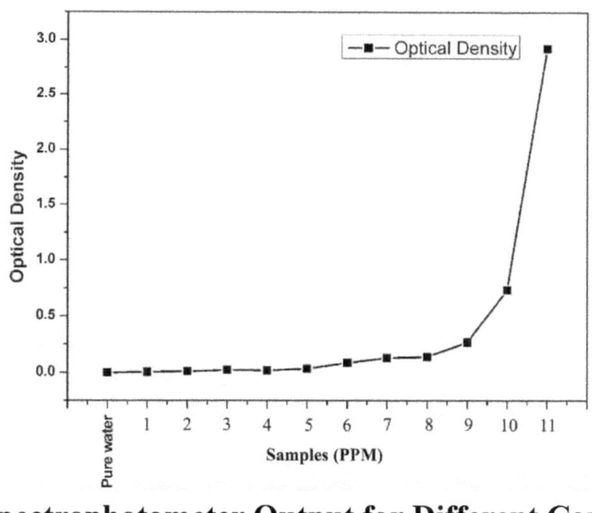

Figure 3.10 Spectrophotometer Output for Different Concentrations of Blue Dye Samples

As the concentration increases, the optical density also increases. Thus, in this case, optical density values have been measured using a spectrophotometer. The prepared dye sample is poured into a glass beaker continuously to measure the color concentration, and the graphs are used to show the sensor's output in all four channels (Blue Filter, Green Filter, Red Filter, and Clear Filter). The graph shown in Figure 3.9 is the output frequency for the different concentrations of blue dye samples in different photodiode channels.

The graph shown in Figure 3.10 gives the output optical density for the different blue dye sample concentrations.

All four modes of photodiode are used during the measurement of color. The selection of mode done using an embedded kit, and all the four-mode frequency outputs are added to measure the color . As the concentration of color changes, the total frequency output also changes.

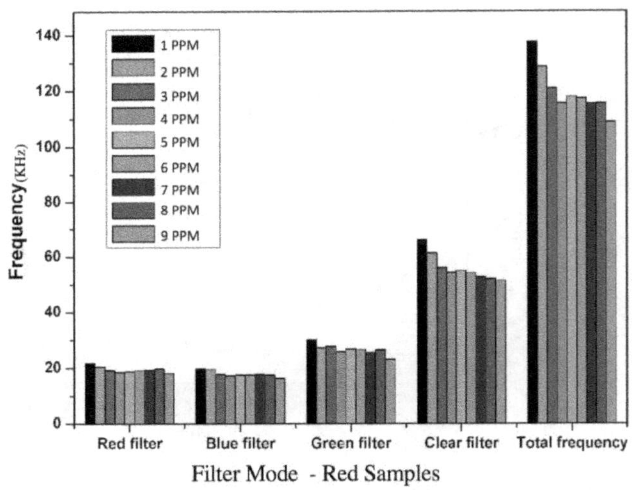

Figure 3.11 Optical Sensor Output for Various Concentrations of Red Samples in Different Channels

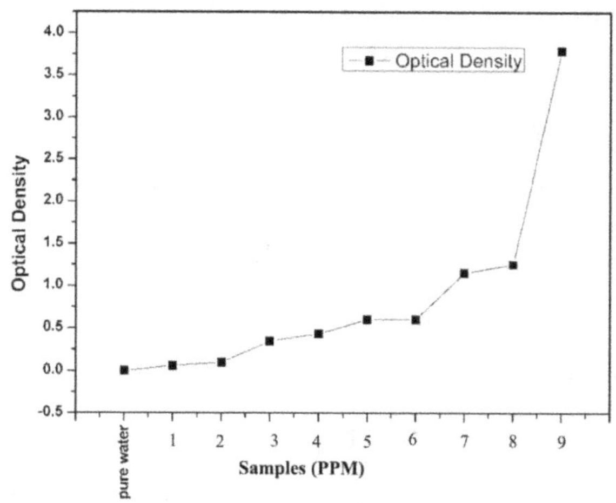

Figure 3.12 Spectrophotometer output for different concentrations of Red dye samples

The graph is shown in Figure 3.11 shows the output frequency for the different concentrations of red dye samples in different photodiode channels & the total frequency of all four modes decreases as the concentration of color samples increases.

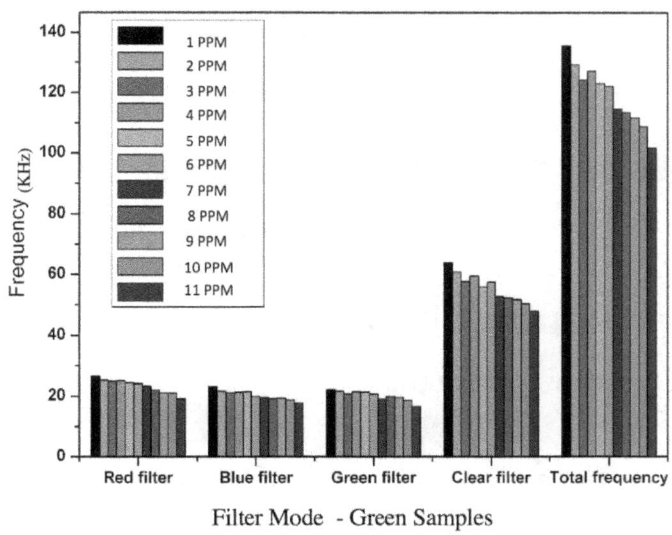

Figure 3.13 Optical sensor output for various concentrations of Green samples in different channels

The graph is shown in Figure 3.12 about the output of optical density values for the different red dye sample concentrations. The graph shown in Figure 3.13 explains the output frequency for the different concentrations of green dye samples in different photodiode channels. The graph is shown in Figure 3.14 about the output of optical density values for the different green dye sample concentrations. For getting high resolution and precious measurement, it has been decided to choose all four channels and take the reading simultaneously. The main advantage of choosing all channels is, the values from all the filters can be obtained and compared to obtain the expected outcome.

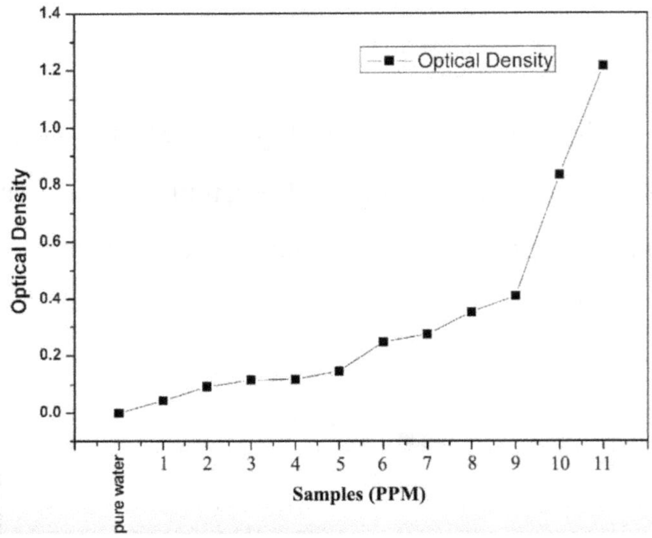

Figure 3.14 Spectrophotometer output for different concentrations of Green dye samples

3.4 CONTROLLER DESIGN

3.4.1 Flow rate optimization

The automated process of decolorization requires an optimum flow rate for the color removal process. Hence a closed-loop system with a TCS3200 as a color sensor, a pump as the actuator, and the PWM signal as the control for operating the pump. The controller was designed to remove the color effectively. The pump was tested with various input voltages to obtain the flow rate. Figure 3.15 shows the various regulated output flow rate for different input voltages. For efficient decolorization, a flow rate of 20ml/min was fixed and regulated by the regulator under the open-loop test. For the closed-loop, PWM signals were generated by the designed controller for effective decolorization.

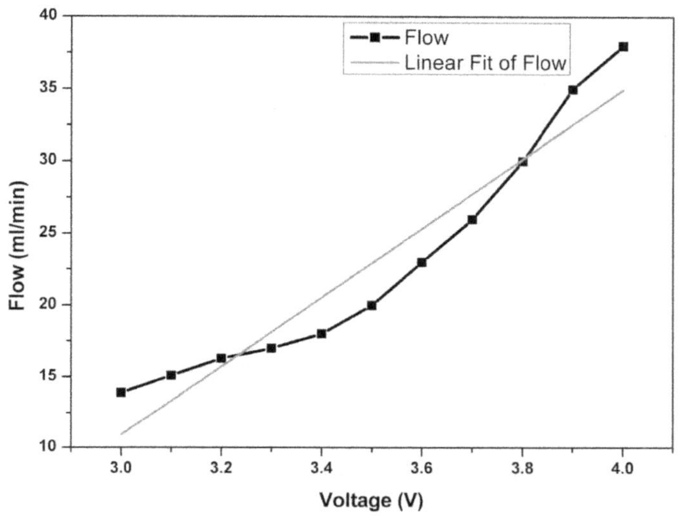

Figure 3.15 Dye Solution Flow Regulation

3.4.2 Open Loop Test

The system an open-loop test, and the decolorizing efficiency was calculated. Under open-loop, a constant flow rate of dye solutions was pumped to the column. From Figure 3.16, it is evident that the decolorizing efficiency goes down after few rounds of decolorization for the PUF matrix. The shelf life of the PUF matrix in decolorizing the dye is estimated in this experiment.

The alginate beads are bound together to form a filter bed. The solution was passed into the column, and the eluates (20ml) were collected at regular time intervals (every 60 minutes). Dye degradation percentage was calculated at the respective time intervals. The efficiency of the alginate beads is proportional to the dye solutions' retention time in the presence of the bacteria. From Figure 3.17, it is evident that the decolorizing efficiency goes down after few rounds of decolorization for alginate beads.

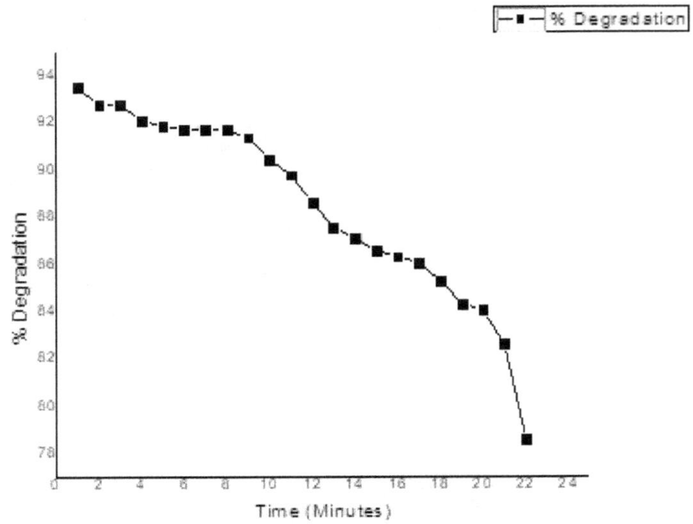

Figure 3.16 Percentage of Color Degradation Results by PUF Method

The SA (Sodium Alginate) beads obtained from the preparation procedure are packed together to form a SA filter. The construction of this experimental setup is entirely different from the PUF setup. In this estimation of SA efficiency, the outlet flow rate is maintained constant, and there is no inlet continuously. The dye solution is poured into the burette. 20ml of decolored samples were collected every one hour. The percentage of degradation values was tabulated. By comparing both of the filters, the PUF removes color much faster than the SA. In the SA reading, the samples were collected for every one hour, but the color changes can be seen drastically in the PUF for every one minute. The colorimeter measured the OD by the wavelength of 517nm. The readings can be plotted in the form of a graph that would be easy to describe the capacity and showing the efficiency of the SA packed beads filter. SA takes more long compared to PUF because the microbes take more time to grow and break the azo bonds present in the dye solution. Figure 3.18 and Figure 3.19 displays the optical density value of degraded sample by PUF method and SA method respectively.

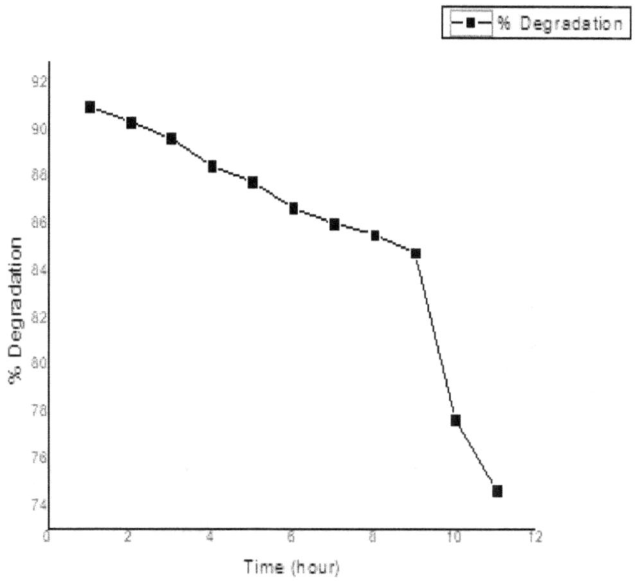

Figure 3.17 Percentage of Color Degradation Results by SA Method

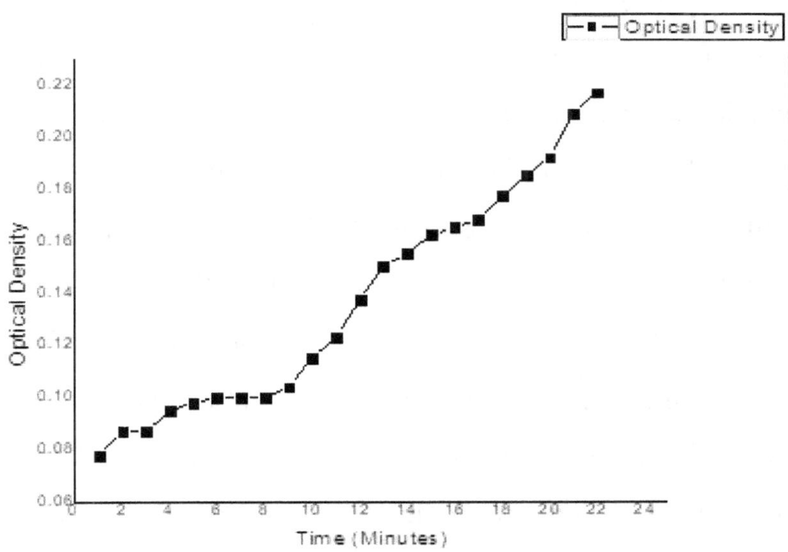

Figure 3.18 Percentage of color degradation (optical density) results by PUF Method

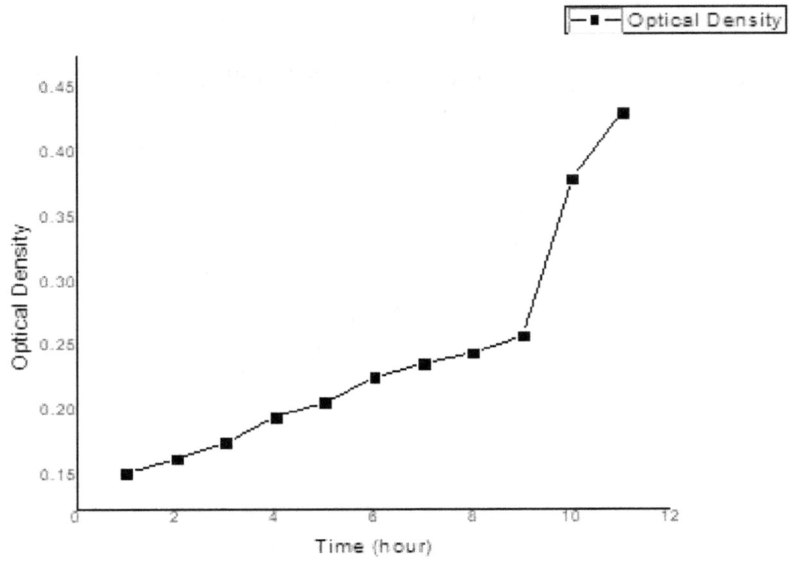

Figure 3.19 Percentage of color degradation (optical density) by SA Method

3.4.3 Closed Loop Test

The whole setup was working in a feedback loop with an apt control algorithm. The experimental setup works in a closed-loop system with a suitable control algorithm implemented in LabVIEW. In the closed-loop system, the output of the process tank, which is expected to be decolorized, is monitored using color sensors to check for any dye present in the solution. The two sensors are arranged so that it measures the presence/absence of the color present in the dye solution. The two sensors are placed before and after the process tank, and the data are collected and compared to conclude how much color is being removed from the dye solution. Based on this data, the PID controller algorithm is implemented in LabVIEW, and does the pump's operation is controlled. The output of the process tank is collected in the settling tank if the dye is completely decolorized. Else the dye solution is fed back into the process tank for further decolorization. Figure 3.20 demonstrates the feedback control system experimental setup for the decolorization process.

This feedback system is made to run continuously to get extreme decolorization.

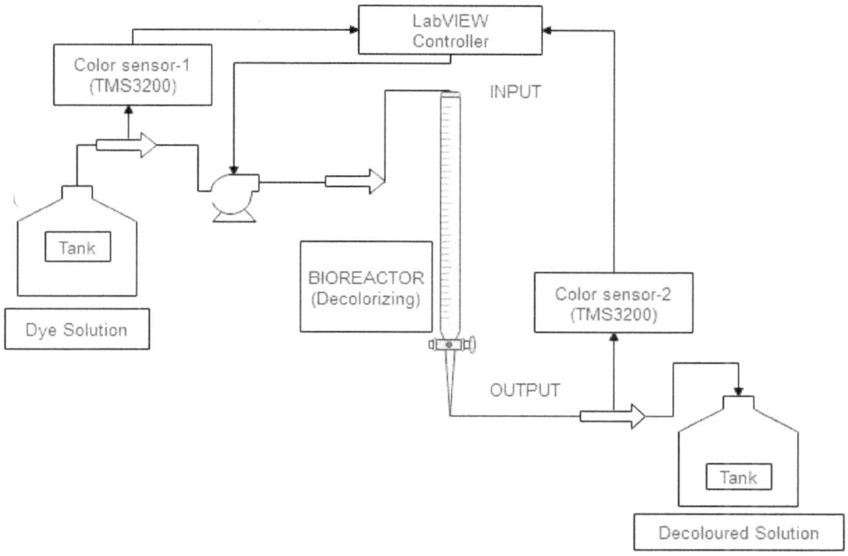

Figure 3.20 Feedback plus Feedforward loop for Color Removal Process

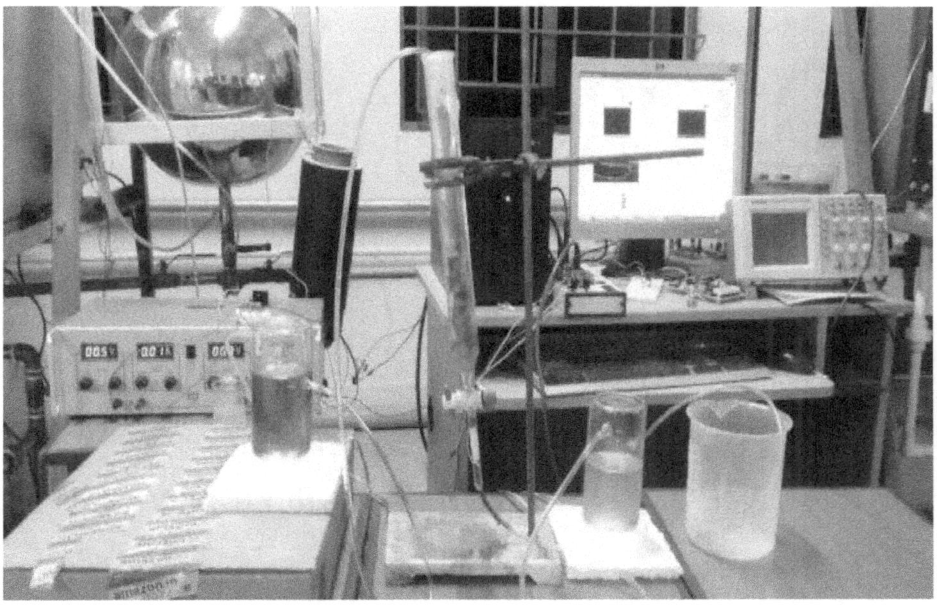

Figure 3.21 Experimental Setup of Color Removal Process

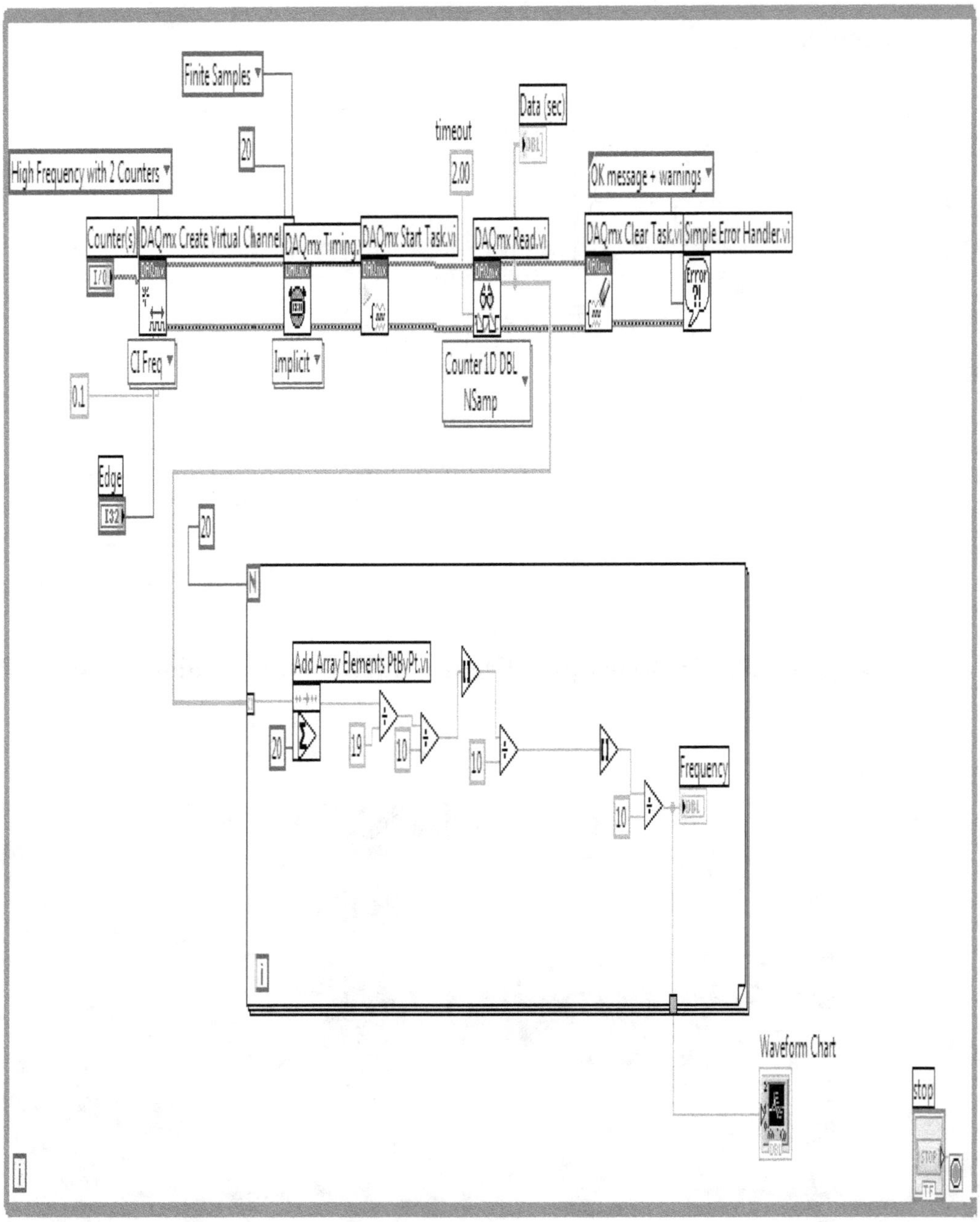

Figure 3.22 Sensor Interfacing (Lab VIEW Block Diagram)

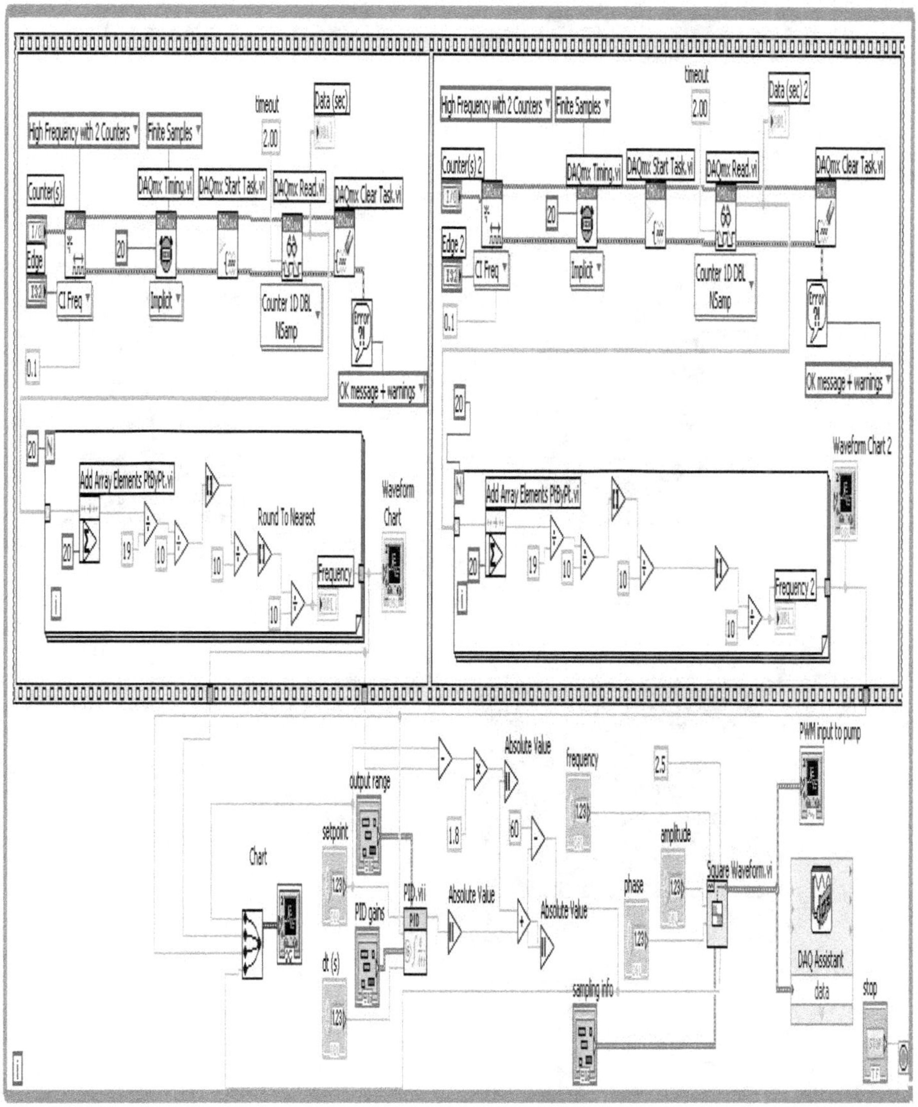

Figure 3.23 Closed Loop (Feedback & Feed Forward) Sensor and Actuator Interface

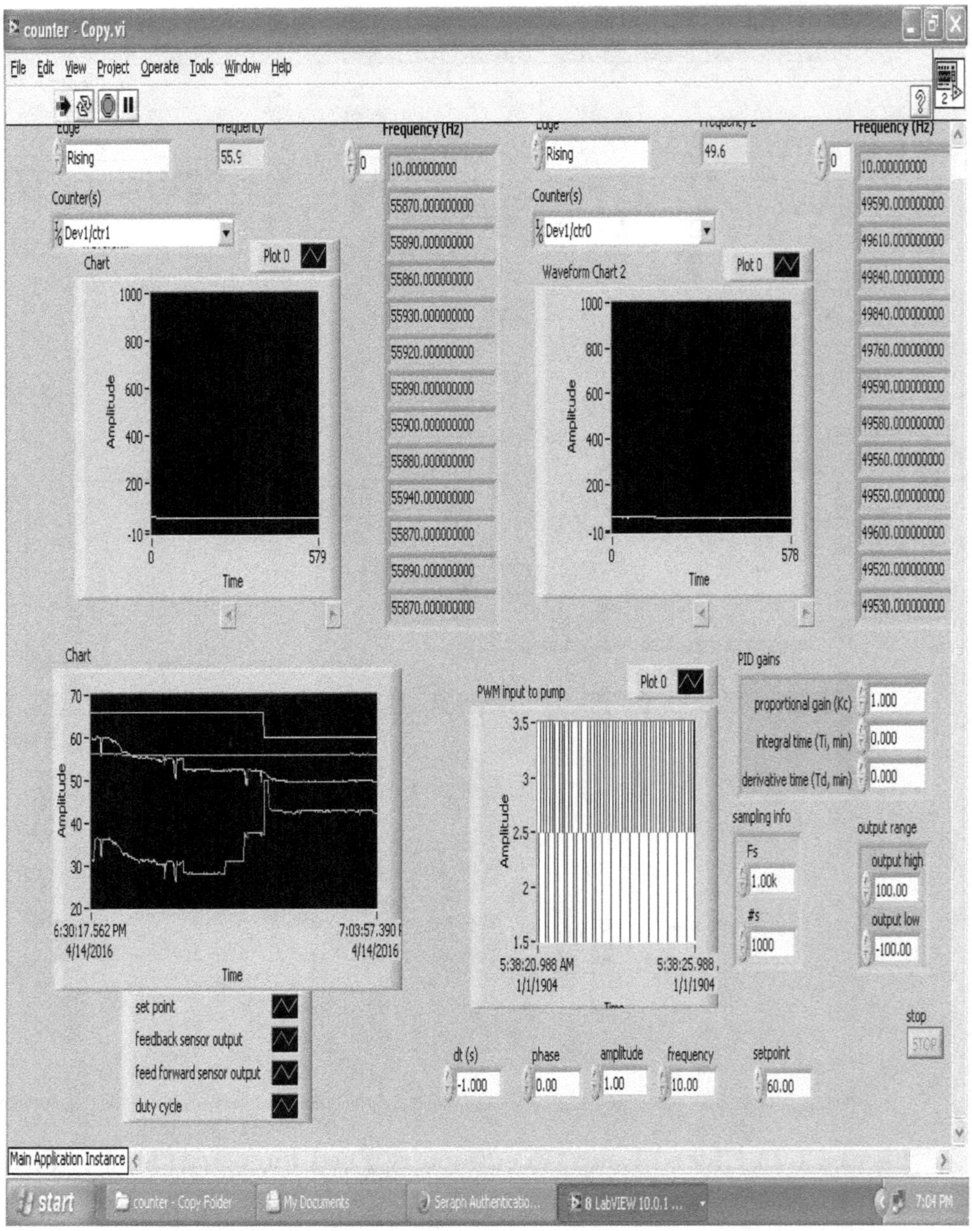

Figure 3.24 Closed Loop (Feedback & Feed Forward) Sensor and Actuator Interface (Front Panel)

The controller produces PWM input to adjust the PUMP. Figure 3.21 shows the experimental setup of color removal process. Figure 3.22 demonstrates LabVIEW block diagram for color sensor interface. Figure 3.23 shows the closed loop (feedback and feed forward) sensor and actuator interface of LabVIEW Block Diagram. Figure 3.24 shows the closed loop (feedback and feed forward) sensor and actuator interface of LabVIEW Front Panel.

3.5 CONCLUSION

The sensor data is acquired via a NI-DAQ in LabVIEW, and the PID control algorithm is implemented to change the pump by PWM circuit. The prime motive of the proposed work to attain the prearranged solution's supreme decolorization is successfully achieved. The effectiveness of the proposed methodology is evaluated by using a similar test offline. The comparison study of the PUF and SA tests was carried out successfully. Nanoparticle immobilized on the polymer gives better decolorization when compared to the sodium alginate immobilized microbes. In this experiments, only a standard volume (1 liter) of the dye solution was tested against the immobilized bacteria and nanoparticles. Further analysis with higher volumes of dye solutions should be done to determine the individual columns' saturation point. Technologies are emerging towards greater heights. As such, this conceptual model is made out to give an efficient way in the decolorization aspect.

There are no consistent methods for measuring color intensity in industrial wastewater, and there is no recognized standard for what color is acceptable in trade waste discharges or recycled water. Generally, there is a lack of consistent information available on color in trade waste, making it problematic to manage the color discharges from individual trade waste customers. This method developed a sensor module that is efficient in monitoring the changes in color intensity in a continuous mode. This method is a newer approach and is cost-effective in comparison to the other methods presently used.

The experimental work has been carried out to demonstrate how a color concentration can be measured continuously. In this work, an optical sensor module is used for monitoring the changes in the concentration of a substance in a continuous fashion. The four-channel photodiode and optical density of the spectrometer are used to design the color measurement of textile effluent water.

Implementation of controller design with suitable control schemes done. Because the complete control can be done on a system operating in a closed-loop only by designing a particular controller, in the batch process, it could not obtain consistent results for the same process. By designing a suitable control algorithm, it obtained a 90% degradation result for the same process, which was 85% before. For increasing the decolorizing efficiency, both the filters must be fused. Flow control made accurate by implementing the PWM input to the pump. For that purpose, the entire process should be done inside the anaerobic chamber, which is also controlled and was made to stop when the decolorizing efficiency of the filters going beyond 90%. This research can be used in any wastewater treatment plant, especially in all textile industries, to avoid environmental pollution.

CHAPTER 4

pH NEUTRALIZATION PROCESS

4.1 INTRODUCTION

In modern years the industrial use of innovative control practices method for the industries has developed additional challenging, generally due to the growing complexity of the developments themselves and improved desires in aspects of product quality and environmental factors. So the process industries need additional consistent, precise, strong, competent& flexible control systems for the process plant's procedure. In order to satisfy the above desires, there is an ongoing need for research on enhanced forms of control. Control of industrial processes is challenging for numerous reasons because of their nonlinear dynamic behavior, uncertain & time-varying parameters, limitations in a manipulated variable, the communication between manipulated and controlled variables, unmeasured and frequent disturbances dead time input, and measurements.

Control of the pH method shows a significant part in dissimilar chemical plants, like wastewater treatment, electrochemistry and precipitation, production of pharmaceuticals, fermentation, and food production such as vegetable oil refining. It's problematic to control a pH process with a satisfactory performance point because of its non-linearity, time-dependence, and sensitivity to small disturbances when working near the correspondence point.

The necessity for pH neutralization in wastewater treatment arises because direct outlet of untreated wastewater would spoil the groundwater and plant growth. Hence the pH neutralization process has to carry out effectively under the open-loop and closed-loop conditions. A methodology to control the pH neutralization process is a very challenging issue due to its nonlinearity. This work focuses on neutralizing the pH value by adding the appropriate amount of Acid and Base solution. More precisely, the pH was controlled in a continuous stirred tank reactor (CSTR). CSTR is a tank in which mixing two solvents in the controlled ratio is conceivable and provided through a stirrer for equivalent mixing. The pH level is controlled by addition NaOH or HCl solution straight into the CSTR. A control mechanism essential part to be applied in demand to regulate the quantity of solution added to compensate for abnormalities in pH correctly.

4.2 STUDY OF pH CHARACTERISTICS

4.2.1 HCl and NaOH Samples Preparation

The samples are prepared using the following formula.

HCl Calculations,

$$Normality\ of\ Hcl\ is\ 11.42 = N_1$$

$$V_1N_1 = V$$

$$V_1 = \frac{V_2N_2}{N_1}$$

$$Volume\ \ V_2 = 100ml$$

$$N_2 = 0.1N$$

$$Hcl\ volume\ V_1 = \frac{100ml \times 0.1N}{11.42N} = 0.88ml\ of\ Hcl$$

The Base (NaOH) solutions are prepared using the calculations given below.

NaOH Calculations,

Table 4.1 Variation in pH value with HCl sample

S. No	HCl (ml)	pH
1	0	11.79
2	1	11.74
3	2	11.67
4	3	11.6
5	4	11.5
6	5	11.38
7	6	11.21
8	7	10.91
9	8	7
10	9	3.08
11	10	2.77
12	11	2.59
13	12	2.46
14	13	2.36
15	14	2.28
16	15	2.21
17	16	2.15
18	17	2.09
19	18	2.04

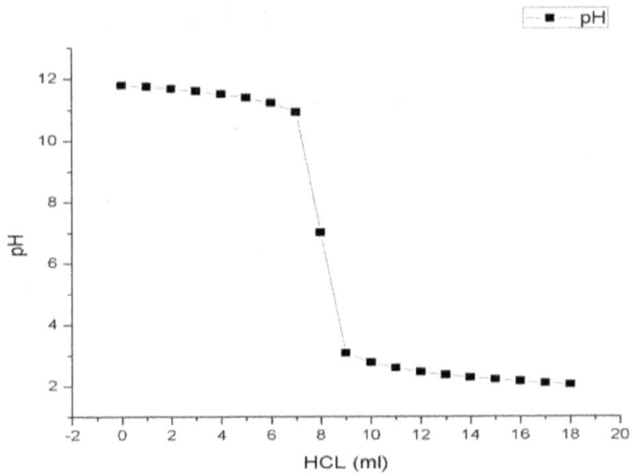

Figure 4.1 Variation in pH value with HCl sample

Figure 4.1 & Table 4.1 shows the changes in pH value for the addition of 1mL of HCl added for each Titration.

Table 4.2 Variation in pH value with NaOH sample

S. No	NaOH (ml)	pH
1	0	2.04
2	1	2.09
3	2	2.15
4	3	2.21
5	4	2.28
6	5	2.36
7	6	2.46
8	7	2.59
9	8	2.77
10	9	3.08
11	10	7
12	11	10.91
13	12	11.21
14	13	11.38
15	14	11.5
16	15	11.6
17	16	11.67
18	17	11.74
19	18	11.79

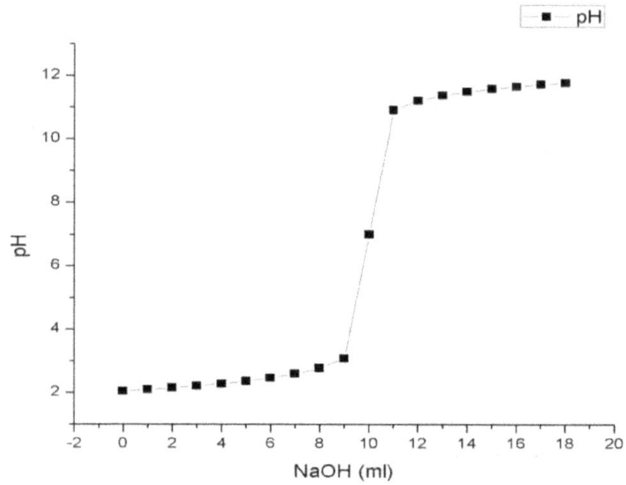

Figure 4.2 Variation in pH value with NaOH sample

Figure 4.2 & Table 4.2 shows the changes in pH value for the addition of 1mL of NaOH added for each Titration. But when the solution's pH range is crossing the limit and approaching seven, even a small amount of addition is showing a considerable variation. Therefore in this place, the controller's role of acid or base motor selection and its speed control becomes necessary.

To test and design the controller system, various solutions is prepared, and several testing are performed. The preparation of solution plays an essential role in the pH neutralization of controller design. Based on the requirement, the solutions are prepared in various concentrations to test. To design the suitable controller, real-time samples are required to test. Along with prepared samples, real-time samples are also collected. The following test is also made in the prepared samples. Testing includes Conductivity test (should be below 500ppm), Nitrate Test (should be below 45ppm), Total suspended solids (0 to 750 mg/l), Sulphate Test (0 to 70mg/l), DO Test, Total hardness, Turbidity (0 to 1000 FAU or NTU). Table 4.3 shows the various test done in the prepared samples.

Table 4.3 Sample Test Results

Test	Sample 1	Sample 2
Conductivity (>500PPM)	1602.56ppm	2931.84ppm
pH	8.175	8.761
Nitrate(>45ppm)	83.67ppm	81.65
Total suspended Solids(0 to 750mg/l)	1067mg/l	706mg/l
Sulphate test (0 to 70mg/l)	80mg/l	81mg/l
DO	4.2mg/l	4.7mg/l
Total Hardness	100mg/l	225mg/l
Turbidity	1100FAU	821FAU

In Table 4.3 reported that the wastewater should be treated before discharge. The above test indicates that the wastewater should undergo these tests before being dispensed for utilization to land or several usages. This work has been regulated only by the pH of the wastewater, thus adding neutralizing solutions into the wastewater to treat. Therefore pH needs to neutralized in wastewater, and treated water can be used for plant irrigation without harming groundwater and plant growth. Figure 4.3 shows the nitrate testing device.

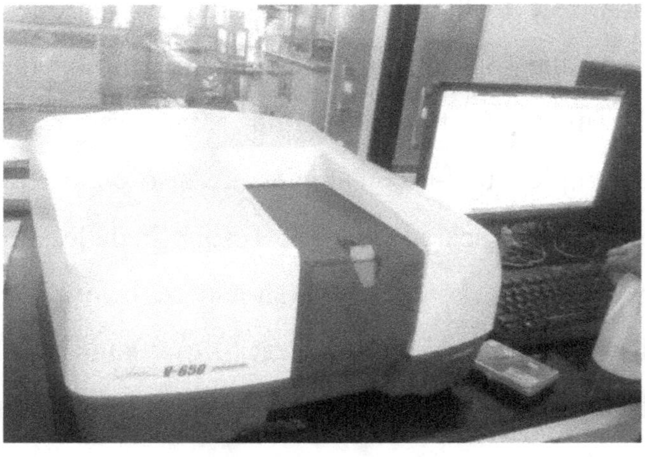

Figure 4.3 Nitrate testing device

4.2.2 pH Sensor Characteristics

In real-time controller design, the electrical output of the pH sensor was obtained and tabulated. Figure 4.4 and Table 4.4 show the plot of pH and the result of pH to understand the sensor's linearity. The pH sensor output is linear, with the pH from 0 to 14.

Table 4.4 pH vs Output of Sensor

S.NO	pH Value	Output (mv)
1	0	414
2	1	355
3	2	296
4	3	237
5	4	177
6	5	118
7	6	59
8	7	0
9	8	-59
10	9	-118
11	10	-177
12	11	-237
13	12	-296
14	13	-355
15	14	-414

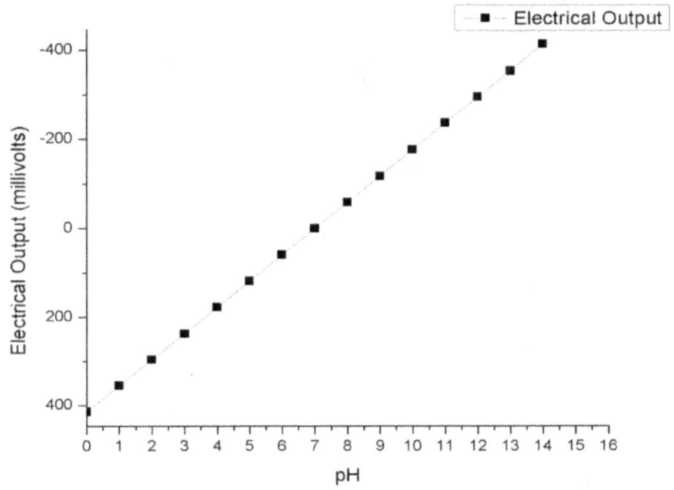

Figure 4.4 Characteristics of pH Sensor (pH vs. mV)

4.3 MATHEMATICAL MODELING

The need for modeling is at increase because of the development of sophisticated simulation tools. Hence the pH neutralization process discussed in this thesis has been modeled using the mass balance equation. Applying transforms to the equations has resulted in a first-order system with gain 3.14 and Time Constant 15.4. The process is considered to have two streams of input and one stream of output. Figure 4.5 shows the process flow diagram of pH Neutralization. Table 4.5 shows the parameters of pH Neutralization process.

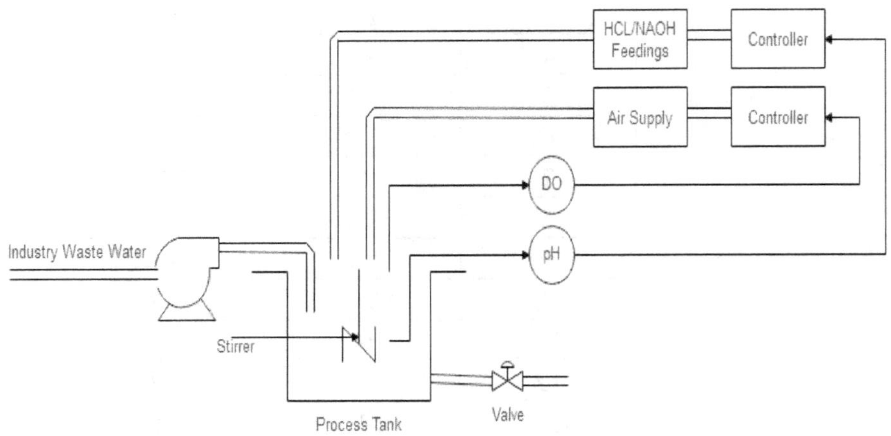

Figure 4.5 Process Flow Diagram of pH Neutralization

a : acid stream with concentration Ca and flow rate Fa

b : base stream with concentration Cb and flow rate Fb

bf : buffer stream with concentration C(bf) and flow rate F(bf)

e : effluent stream with concentration Ce and flow rate Fe

Temperature maintains 25 degree Celsius

Density, $\rho = \rho a = \rho b = \rho bf = \rho e$

Total mass balance:

Accumulation of total mass in the tank/time = [total input to the tank/time] – [total output from the tank/time]

$$\frac{d}{dt}\rho v = \rho aFa + \rho bFb + \rho(bf)F(bf) + \rho eFe \tag{4.1}$$

Based on assumption

$$\frac{d}{dt}v = fa + fb + f(bf) \qquad - fe \tag{4.2}$$

The balance on the component:

Accumulation of particular component in the tank/time = [total input of the element to the tank/time] – [total output from the tank]

$$\frac{d}{dt}(co, v) = [ca.fa + cb.fb + c(bf).f(bf)] - ce.fe \tag{4.3}$$

$$v.\frac{d}{dt}(co) + co.\frac{d}{dt}(v) = [ca.fa + cb.fb + c(bf).f(bf)] - ce.fe \tag{4.4}$$

$$v.\frac{d}{dt}(co) + co.[fa + fb + f(bf) - fe] = [ca.fa + cb.fb + c(bf).f(bf)] - ce.fe$$

$$v.\frac{d}{dt}(co) = -co.[fa + fb + f(bf) - fe] + [ca.fa + cb.fb + c(bf).f(bf)] - ce.fe$$

$$v.\frac{d}{dt}(co) = \{ca.fa - co.fa + cb.fb - co.fb + c(bf).f(bf) - co.f(bf) - ce.fe + co.fe\}$$

$$v.\frac{d}{dt}(co) = (ca - co)fa + (cb - co)fb + (c(bf) - co)f(bf) - (ce - co)fe \tag{4.5}$$

According to the assumption that the stirrer in the CSTR well stirring takes place. The automatic process flow diagram of Ph neutralization is shown in Figure 4.5. Hence the concentration of solution inside the tank and in the effluent stream is same

Hence Ce = Co

$$v.\frac{d}{dt}(co) = (ca - co)fa + (cb - co)fb + (c(bf) - co)f(bf)$$

Taking Laplace transform of the above equation

$$vs.co(s) = (ca - co(s))fa(s) + (cb - co(s))fb(s) + (c(bf) - co(s))f(bf)(s)$$

$$\frac{co(s)}{fb(s)} = \frac{\{2.cb + \frac{c(bf).F(bf).ca}{fa.cb}\}}{\{vs + fa\left[1 + \frac{ca}{cb}\right] + f(bf)\}} \quad (4.6)$$

Table 4.5 Parameters of the neutralization process

$(C_{HNO3})a = 0.003M$	$(C_{HNO3})b = 0M$	$(C_{HNO3})C = 0M$
$(C_{NaHNO3})a = 0M$	$(C_{NaHNO3})b = 0.03M$	$(C_{NaHNO3})c = 0.0005M$
$(C_{NaOH})a = 0M$	$(C_{NaOH})b = 0M$	$(C_{NaOH})c = 0.003M$
$Fa = 16.6\ mL/s$	$Fb = 0.55\ mL/s$	$Fc = 15.5\ mL/s$
$W_{1a} = 0.003M$	$W_{1b} = 0.0M$	$W_{1c} = 0.00035M$
$W_{2a} = 0M$	$W_{2a} = 0.03M$	$V = 2900ML$
$pK1 = 6.35$	$pK2 = 10.25$	$pH = 7.00$

Substituting Table 4.5 parameters in the equation 4.6 then the transfer function will be

$$\frac{Coutput(s)}{fbase(s)} = Gp(s)$$

$$Transfer\ Function = Gp(s) = \frac{3.14}{(15.4\ s + 1)}$$

4.4 PID CONTROLLER DESIGN USING SIMULATION

Controllers are used in a closed-loop control system. The closed-loop control system automatically manipulates the output based on the difference between the feedback signals and the reference signal. The controller is an element used to produce manipulated variables from the error variable for control action. A proportional integral derivative controller (PID controller) is a standard control loop feedback mechanism (controller) extensively used in industrial control systems a PID is a maximum frequently applied feedback controller. A PID controller analyses an "error" significance as the variance between a measured process variable and the desired set point. The controller efforts to reduce the error by regulating the method control inputs.

The PID controller scheming (procedure) includes three distinct constant parameters and is consequently occasionally called three-term control: the proportional, the integral, and derivative values, designated P, I, and D. Heuristically, these principles can be interpreted in terms of time: P depends on the present error, I on the accumulation of previous errors, and D is an estimate of future errors, based on the present rate of variation. The weighted sum of these three arrangements is used to regulate the process via a control component such as a control valve situation or the power provided to a heating component. Figure 4.6 demonstrates the simulation design of the PID controller using MATLAB.

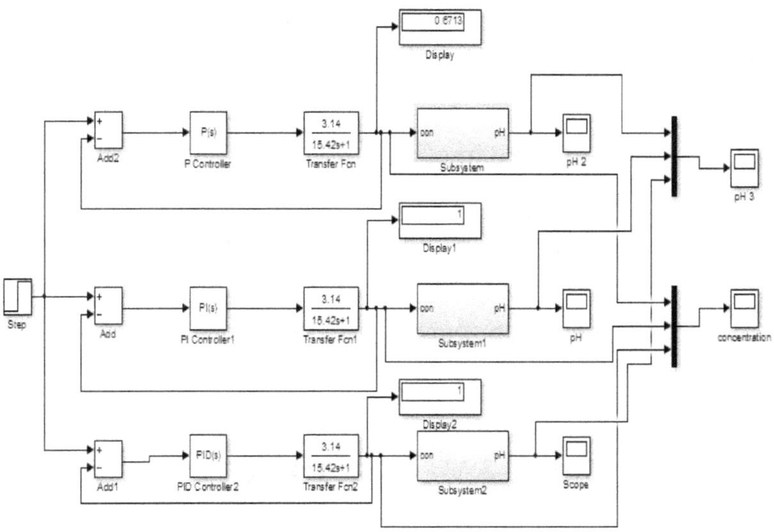

Figure 4.6 Simulation of PID Controller using MATLAB

A frequency domain approach is followed for the closed-loop system.

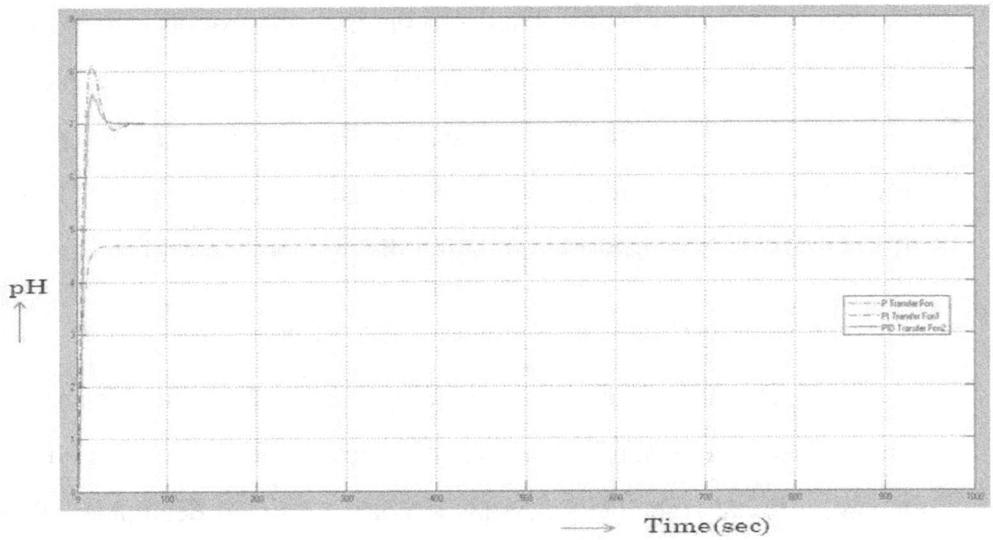

Figure 4.7 Response of P, PI, PID Controller

Figure 4.7 shows the response of P, PI, PID Controller. The performance criteria of various parameters such as settling time, Integral Absolute Error (IAE), and Integral Square Error (ISE) are given in Table 4.6.

Table 4.6 Performance criteria results for PID

S. No	Parameters	PID controller
1	Settling Time(sec)	60
2	Integral Absolute Error (IAE)	69.21
3	Integral Square Error (ISE)	291.3

4.5 REAL-TIME IMPLEMENTATION OF PID CONTROLLER

Wastewater is sent through the sand filter, and gravel for the filtering process then passed into the settling tank from where it is given to the process tank. Here, the pH of the process tank is the output variable, the flow rate of the acid, and the base solution's flow rate is the manipulated variable. The pH value of the process tank should be controlled at the desired value. So, the controller is designed for the non-linear system and implemented using Lab VIEW software.

The pH sensor is an electrode that is dipped in the process tank. The output of the sensor is in the mV range. The sensor information is developed through DAQ to LabVIEW. Based on the sensor data, the PID controller generates the necessary control signal to the driver circuit, which controls the flow rate of acid and base tank. Therefore the addition of acid and base will achieve maintaining the pH of the solution. Figure 4.8 shows the block diagram of the pH neutralization technique.

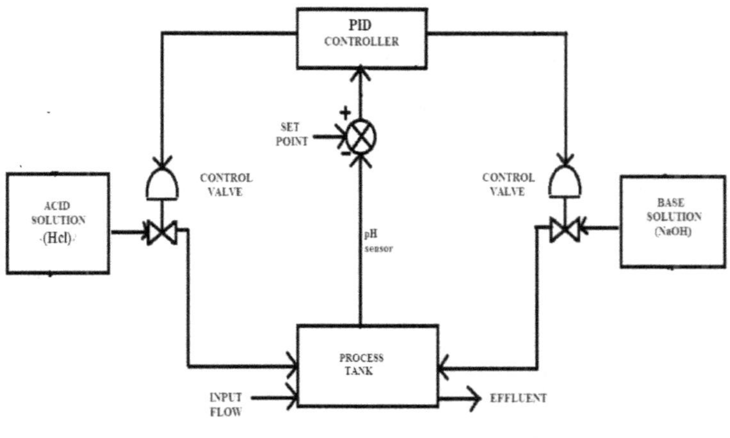

Figure 4.8 Block diagram of pH control system

PID design was performed in real-time using the LabVIEW platform. The reason for choosing LabVIEW is because of its versatility and simple steps in interfacing with hardware. The experiment is carried out using case structure enum for the usage of 3 cases, i.e., when the pH of the process is greater than 7 case-a structure is used for the addition of base (NAOH), when less than seven than case-b structure is used for acid (HCl) addition and final case-c executed when pH is equal to 7 for no action. The output is feed to hardware through DAQ assistant.

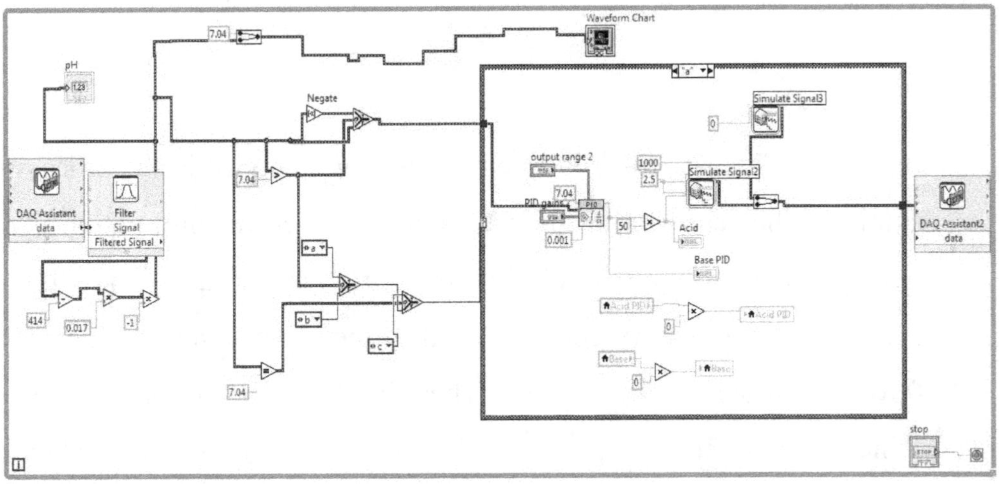

Figure 4.9 PID Controller Design using LabVIEW to add NaOH (If pH > 7)

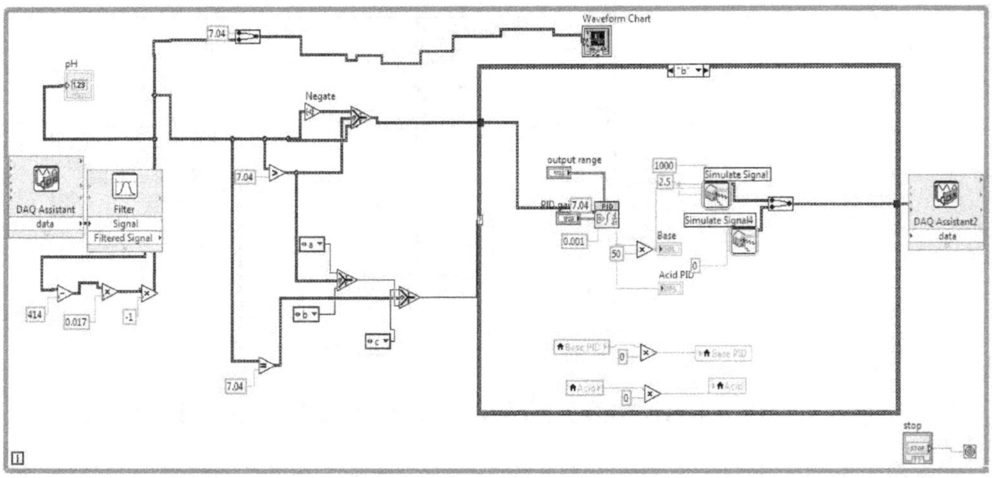

Figure 4.10 PID Controller Design Using LabVIEW to Add HCl

(If pH < 7)

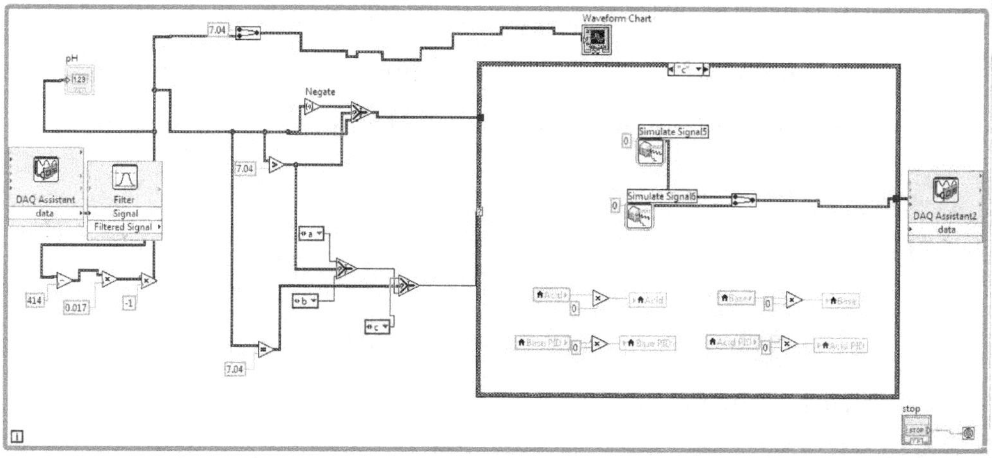

Figure 4.11 PID Controller Design using LabVIEW for Neutral (If pH = 7)

Figure 4.9 shows the LabVIEW diagram for the addition of NaOH solution (pH > 7). Figure 4.10 demonstrates the LabVIEW diagram for addition of HCl solution (pH < 7). Figure 4.11 shows LabVIEW for Neutral (pH = 7), where no control action is required.

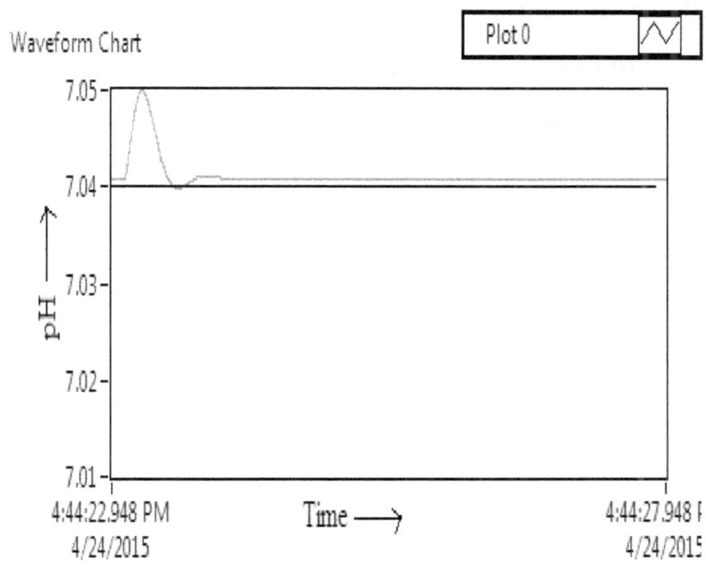

Figure 4.12 Response of pH Neutralization Process

Figure 4.12 show the results of the real-time control system for the Neutralization process. The results show that the controller performance is better in terms of settl.ing time and oscillations.

4.6 CONCLUSION

The experimental setup of pH neutralization gives the Control problems of the process several difficulties mainly due to their highly nonlinear characteristics. The conventional PID controller was designed and implemented in simulation. The settling time, integral absolute error, and integral square error were studied for the controllers were studied. A real-time PID controller was designed in such a way that the system is physically realizable and works very fast to neutralize pH.

The solution was prepared with 0.1 N normality of HCl, but when the volume of solution in the process increases, normality is to be increased to achieve better control. Therefore pH neutralized wastewater is treated and used for plant irrigation without harming both groundwater and plant growth.

CHAPTER 5

REAL-TIME IMPLEMENTATION OF DISSOLVED OXYGEN CONTROL PROCESS

The Dissolved Oxygen (DO) is considered an essential factor in measuring water quality. The dissolved oxygen level in the water should be at right amounts for the aquatic life in the water. The presence of dissolved oxygen is mandatory for the aquatic level, however the range should be above 5PPM. Continuously changing amount of dissolved oxygen in the water level affects aquatic life and pollute the nominal rate of the water which should be processed. Less amount of dissolved oxygen also causes water pollution. The cloudy appearance of the water causes the presence of suspended and colloidal matter. In the waterworks field, a turbidity measurement is used to indicate the clarity of the water. The proposed system suggests a method of measuring turbidity, dissolved oxygen, and designing an efficient DO controller. Since turbidity is inversely proportional to the DO value of water, this research contributes an enhanced approach of model-free control for dissolved oxygen.

5.1 CHARACTERISTICS OF DISSOLVED OXYGEN

Dissolved oxygen (DO) is a parameter that is required to monitor water quality. This is because many chemical and biological reactions in water are dependant directly or indirectly on available oxygen.

Dissolved oxygen is the level of free, non-compound oxygen present in water or other liquids. It is an essential parameter in assessing water quality because it influenced the organisms living in the water body. A dissolved oxygen level that is too high or too low can disturb aquatic life and affect water quality. Non-compound oxygen, or free oxygen (O_2), is oxygen that is not bonded to any other element. Dissolved oxygen is the presence of these free O_2 molecules within the water. The bonded oxygen molecule in water (H_2O) is in a compound and does not count towards dissolved oxygen levels. The free oxygen molecules dissolve in water, much like salt or sugar when it is stirred.

Dissolved oxygen is necessary for fish, invertebrates, bacteria, and plants. These organisms use oxygen in respiration, just as organisms on land. Fish acquire oxygen for respiration through their gills, whereas plant life and phytoplankton need dissolved oxygen for respiration when there is no light for photosynthesis. The amount of dissolved oxygen needed changes from creature to creature. Bottom feeders, crabs, oysters, and worms require a minimal amount of oxygen (1-6 mg/L), whereas shallow water fish need higher levels (4-15 mg/L). Microbes, for example, bacteria and fungi also need dissolved oxygen. These organisms utilise DO decompose organic material at the bottom of a water body. Microbial decomposition is an important contributor to nutrient recycling. But suppose there is a large amount of decaying organic material (from dying algae and other organisms) in a water body with infrequent or no turnover (also known as stratification). In that case, the oxygen at lower water level gets used up quicker.

5.2 MEASUREMENT SYSTEM DESCRIPTION

Turbidity and dissolved oxygen are inversely related to each other. The more turbidity, the less dissolved oxygen there is for living organisms to breathe, negatively affecting animal populations. Human impact has played an major role in keeping the turbidity levels high in these water samples.

5.2.1 Turbidity Measurement

The turbidity values are measured in NTU (Nephelometric Unit). This method is recommended to measure the intensity of the light transmitted through the sample. It includes a light source, a LASER emitting diode at a wavelength of 670nm. The light from the LASER passes through the turbid solution and falls on a photodetector. The photodetector's output signal is given as analog input to the microprocessor and then calibrated to show NTU with the minimum and maximum value shown in Table 5.1. This designed turbidity meter values are compared with the standard turbidity measuring instrument for standardization. Figure 5. 1 shows the block diagram to measure the turbidity.

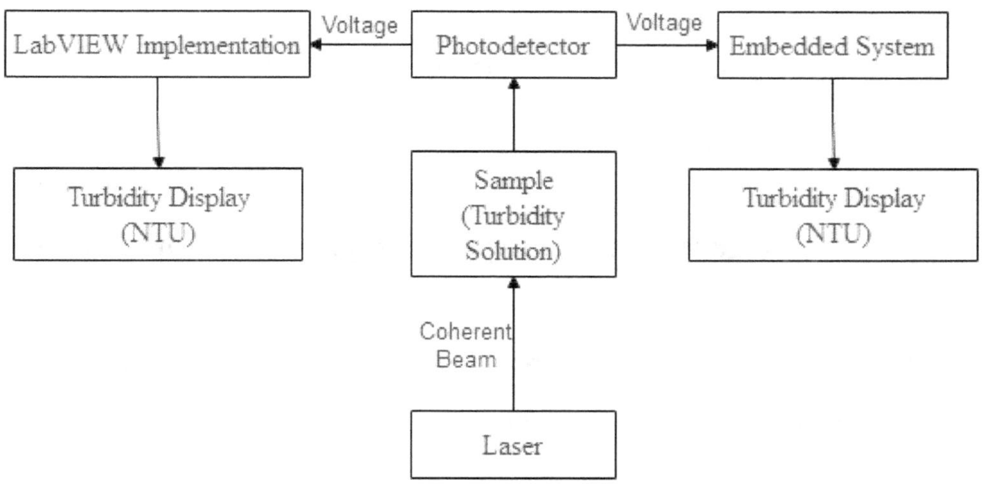

Figure 5.1 Turbidity Measurement Block Diagram

Table 5.1 Min and Max Output Voltage value of Turbidity Measurement

SOLUTION (NTU)	VOLTAGE (volts)
40	0.3
400	4.6

5.2.1.1 Solution Preparation

To calibrate the turbidity measuring system, different known NTU samples were prepared. The standard formazin [20] (heterocyclic polymer) is organized by three-step processes.

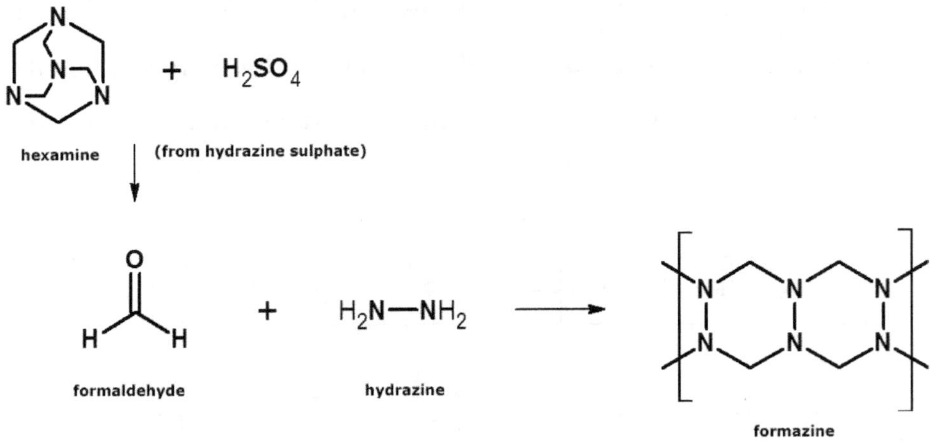

Figure 5.2 Three steps of Sample Solution preparation

Step 1 - Preparation of solution A: Dissolving 1 gm of Hydrazine sulfates in 50ml of water and dilute to 100ml using distilled water.

Step 2 – Preparation of solution B: Dissolving 10 gm of Hexamine in 50ml of distilled water and diluting 100ml in distilled water.

Step 3 - Formazin Preparation: Take 5ml of solution A and mix it with 5ml of solution B and stand for 24 hours at 25 ° C to 30° C temperature and dilute to

100ml of distilled water to attain a standard formazin turbid solution of 400NTU. The stock samples were analyzed and tested to calibrate the measuring system. The chemical reactions are shown in Figure 5. 2.

5.2.1.2 Measurement of Turbidity using LabVIEW Program

The results have been acquired from the turbidity sensor using the known samples which were prepared. The analog voltage from the turbidity sensor is given as variable input through the DAQ in LabVIEW to the formula node. The formula node evaluates the turbidity value and which is displayed on the front panel. The results were revealed in the embedded LED display and in LabVIEW. Using formula node, DAQ, and While loop in LabVIEW is used to convert the LED voltage (0-5V) output to Nephelometric (40-400 NTU) Unit. Figure 5.3 shows the LabVIEW program for converting Voltage to NTU.

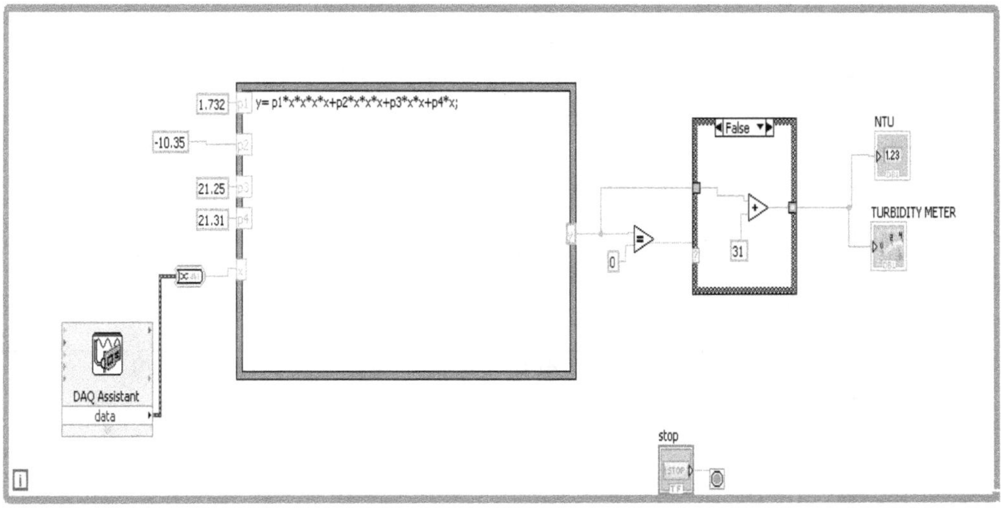

Figure 5.3 LabVIEW for converting Voltage to NTU

Higher order polynomial equation can improve the curve fitting the relation between input (voltage) and output (turbidity). Hence, 4th degree linear polynomial formula which is used to convert voltage into turbidity as follows:

$$Y = q1*x^4 + q2*x^3 + q3*x^2 + q4*x + q5 \quad (5.1)$$

$q1 = 1.732$

$q2 = -10.35$

$q3 = 21.25$

$q4 = 21.31$

$q5 = 31$

Table 5.2 Measurement of Turbidity for Various Known Samples

S. NO	STANDARD SOLUTION (NTU)	VOLTAGE (VOLTS)
1	40	0.3
2	55	0.86
3	86	1.39
4	128	2.74
5	146	3
6	200	3.6
7	228	3.94
8	323	4.52
9	345	4.6
10	375	4.7
11	400	4.8

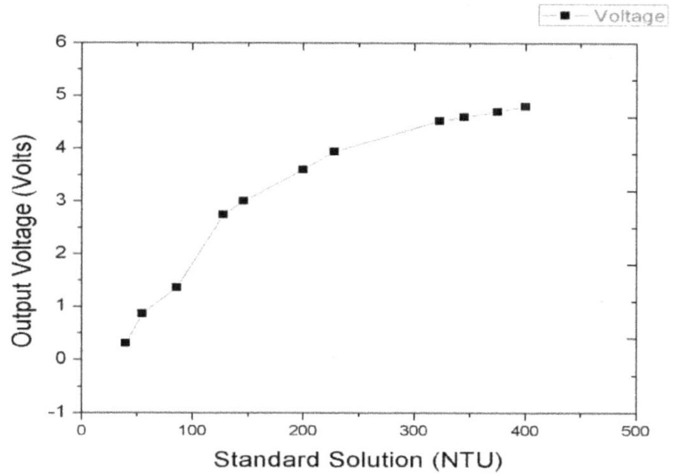

Figure 5.4 Measurement of Turbidity for Various Known Samples

Table 5.2 reports that output voltage for ten known samples. Figure 5.4 shows the output voltage for ten known samples with different turbidity.

5.2.2 Dissolved Oxygen Measurement Setup

In the DO measurement setup DO ranges from 0-40ppm, and the temperature ranges from $(0\text{-}50)^0$ C. The following steps involve the DO sensor system calibration. Figure 5.5 shows the changes in DO value with respect to temperature.

5.2.2.1 DO Probe Assembly

1. Fit the membrane on the lower part of the electrolyte tube, be careful to handle its membrane
2. Fix the ring on the electrolyte tube covering the sides of the membrane
3. Fill KCl solution 7.5% in the electrolyte tube to its top.

4. Insert the electrode in the electrolyte tube and tightly screw it up. Now the probe is ready to use.

5.2.2.2 DO Meter Procedure

1. Set the temperature knob to the solution temperature to calibrate the knob to the extreme right position and zero knobs to the extreme left position.
2. Place the DO probe in 2% sodium sulfide solution.
3. Allow the display to attain equilibrium.
4. Set the knob zero to bind the display to read 00.0by keeping the temp knob to the solution's actual temp.
5. Calibrate knob should be at the extreme right position.
6. Now calibrate the instrument with the known value of DO solution.
7. Take 250 ml flask and fill 2/3 of it with distilled water.
8. Stopper the flask and shank it for 20 secs.
9. Remove the stopper and swirl the water back and repeat the procedure four times.
10. Measure the water's temp and set the temp knob to the temp of the water in the tank.

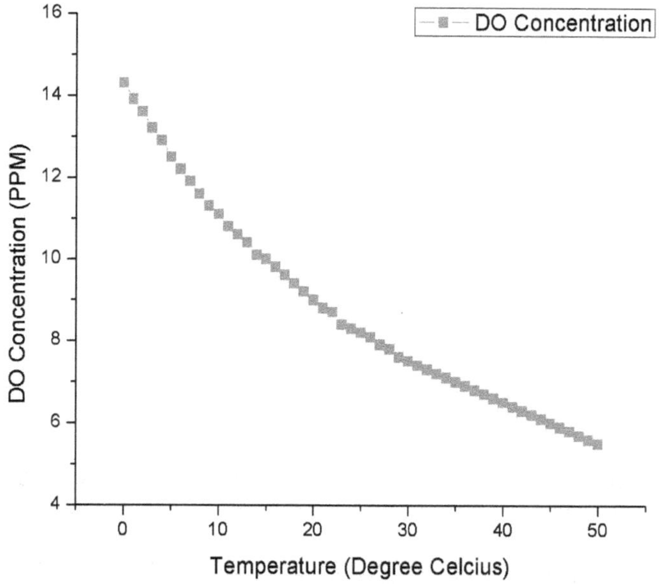

Figure 5.5 Temperature vs. DO

5.3 DISSOLVED OXYGEN AERATION PROCESS SETUP

The real-time PID controller is implemented in LabVIEW to control the aeration process. Three samples of 30L quantity, including domestic wastewater, paper industry wastewater, and drinking water, were taken for experimental study. The setpoint was fixed to 5 PPM, and the PID controller designed in LabVIEW tuned using the Zigler Nichols method was used to control the aeration process to obtain the desired set point. The air pump is used for the aeration process. The PWM signal from the processor is given to the L298N driver circuit. The driver circuit then drives the air pump in the range between 0-12v. According to the controlled signal, the voltage supply is given to the air pump and the driver circuit. Fig 5.6 shows the overall block diagram of Dissolved oxygen aeration process control in the effluent wastewater.

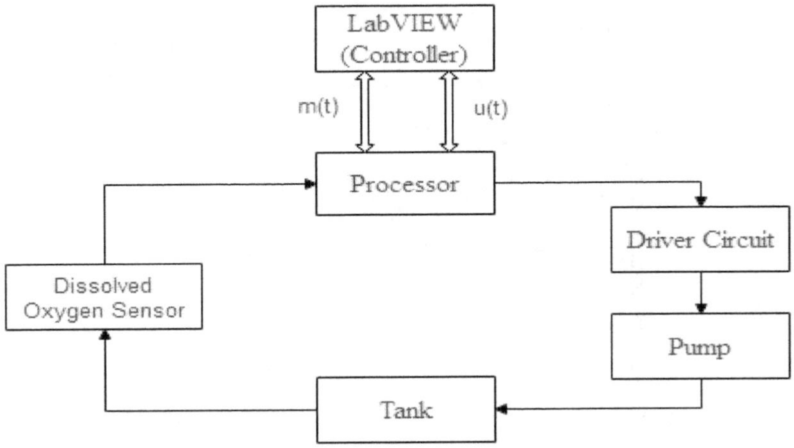

Figure 5.6 Schematic Diagram of Dissolved oxygen aeration process control

The dissolved oxygen sensor works based on the amperometric method. The current flow in between the electrodes is proportional to the dissolved oxygen concentration in the water. The analog output from the dissolved oxygen sensor is interfaced with embedded processor. In order to acquire the data in LabVIEW, the embedded processor act as DAQ. The air pump is used as an actuator device to adjust the DO level in the wastewater by varying the pump's input voltage range from 0-12v.

Table 5.3 Experimental data of Aeration Tank DO value with 2V Input to pump

Time(sec)	DO (ppm)	mV
0	3.2	32.1
30	3.6	36.3
60	3.9	39.3
90	4.2	42.1
120	4.5	44.8
150	4.8	47.5
180	5.1	50.2
210	5.4	52.8
240	5.6	55.1

Table 5.3 (Continued)

270	5.8	57.4
300	6	59.4
330	6.2	61.5
360	6.4	36
390	6.6	64.7
420	6.7	65.9
450	6.9	67.4
480	7	68.4
510	7.1	69.5
540	7.2	70.4
570	7.3	71.3
600	7.4	72
630	7.4	72.6
660	7.5	73.3
690	7.5	73.8
720	7.6	74.2
750	7.6	74.7
780	7.7	75.1
810	7.7	75.3
840	7.7	75.7
870	7.8	75.9
900	7.8	76.1
930	7.8	76.2
960	7.8	76.4
990	7.8	76.6
1020	7.8	76.8
1050	7.9	76.9
1080	7.9	77
1110	7.9	77.1
1140	7.9	77.1
1170	7.9	77.1

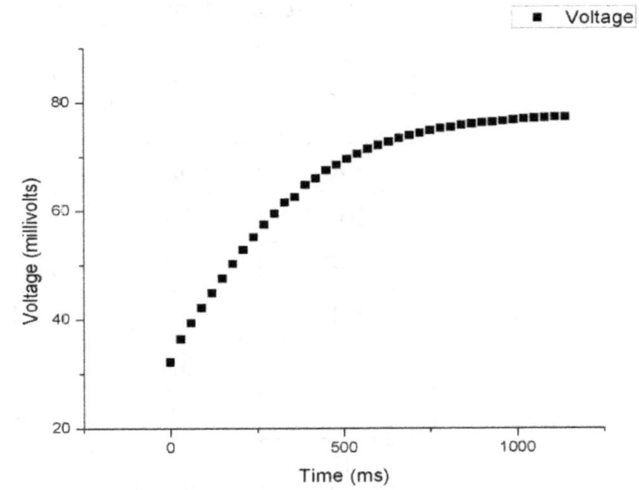

Figure 5.7 Open Loop Response of DO (Voltage) Sensor with 2V Input to Pump

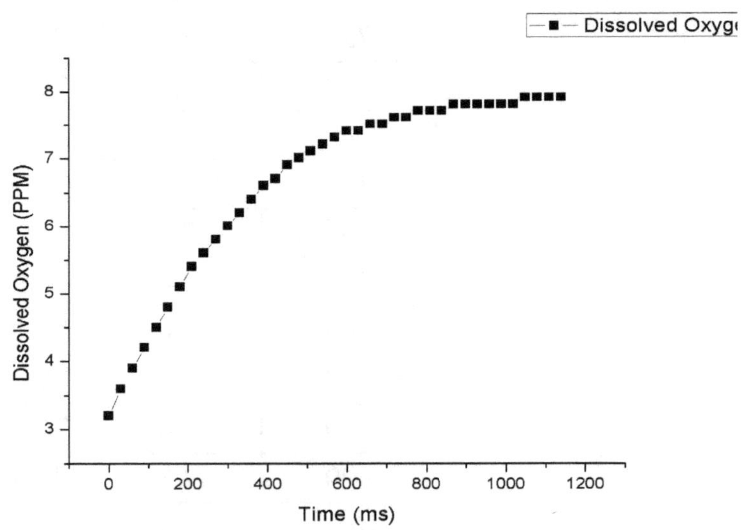

Figure 5.8 Open Loop Response of DO (PPM) Sensor with 2V Input to Pump

Figure 5.7 & 5.8 shows the response of the pump for the 2V Input concerning time. Form these responses its inferred that the DO value increases with repect to time and reaches saturation at 8 PPM for 2V as the input voltage.

Table 5.3 depicts the DO value reaction in the aeration tank in the 2V input to the Air pump.

Table 5.4 Experimental data of Aeration Tank DO value with 4V Input to pump

Time (sec)	DO (ppm)	mV
0	1	10
30	1.6	16
60	2.9	28
90	4	39
120	5	49
150	5.7	55
180	6.3	61
210	7	68
240	7.7	74
270	8.5	82
300	9.8	95
330	10	96
360	10.2	99
390	10.6	106
420	11	108
450	11.1	108
480	11.2	109
540	11.2	110
570	11.2	110
600	11.3	111
630	11.3	111
660	11.4	111
690	11.4	112
720	11.5	112

Table 5.4 (Continued)

750	11.4	113
780	11.5	114
810	11.5	114
840	11.6	114
870	11.7	116
900	11.8	118
930	12	116
960	12	116
990	12.0	117
1020	12.1	118
1050	12	118
1080	12.1	118
1110	12.1	119
1140	12	119
1170	12	119
1200	12.1	119
1230	12.1	119
1260	12.1	120
1290	11.9	120
1320	11.9	121
1350	12.5	121
1380	12.4	120
1410	12.4	119
1440	12.4	120
1470	12.4	121
1500	12.4	120

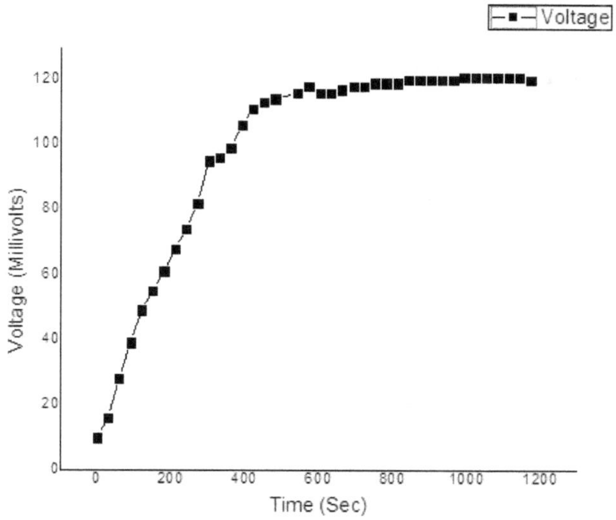

Figure 5.9 Open Loop Response of DO (Voltage) Sensor with 4V Input to Pump

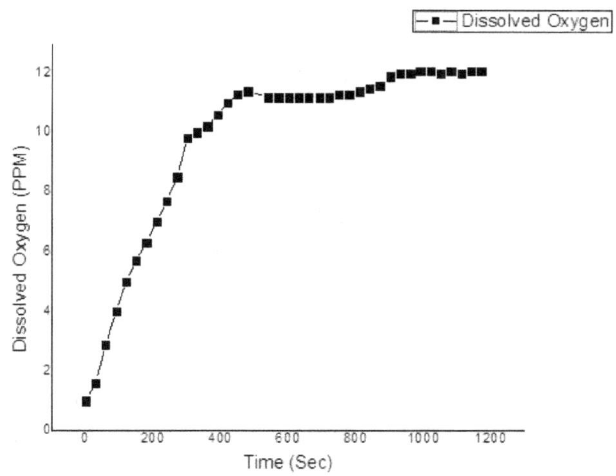

Figure 5.10 Open Loop Response of DO (PPM) Sensor with 4V Input to Pump

Figure 5.9 & 5.10 demonstrates the response of the pump for the 4V Input concerning time. Form these responses its inferred that the DO value increases with repect to time and reaches saturation at 12 PPM for 4V as the input voltage Table 5.4 represents the DO value response in the aeration tank in the 4V input to the Air pump.

Table 5.5 Experimental data of Aeration Tank DO value with 10V Input to pump

Time (sec)	DO (ppm)	mV
0	9.4	94.6
30	9.5	95.2
60	10.5	105.4
90	10.6	105.8
120	10.8	108.1
150	11.2	114.6
180	13	130
210	14.4	142
240	13.1	128.5
270	13.3	132
300	14	138.3
330	14.5	140.6
360	14.6	145.9
390	14.7	147.2
420	14.4	147.3
450	14.8	147.9
480	14.7	147.5
510	14.7	147.2
540	14.7	147.1

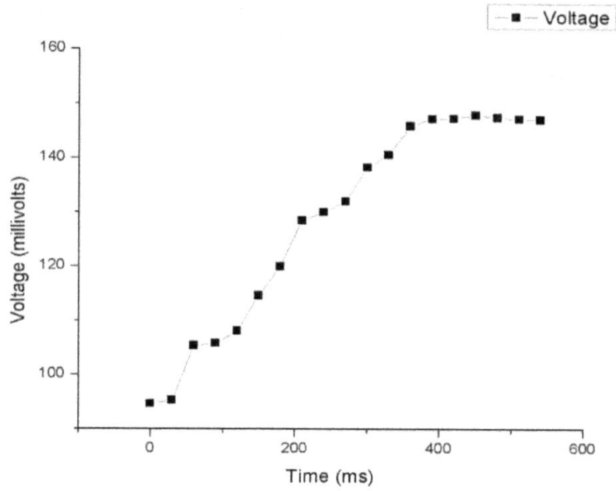

Figure 5.11 Open Loop Response of DO (Voltage) Sensor with 10V Input to Pump

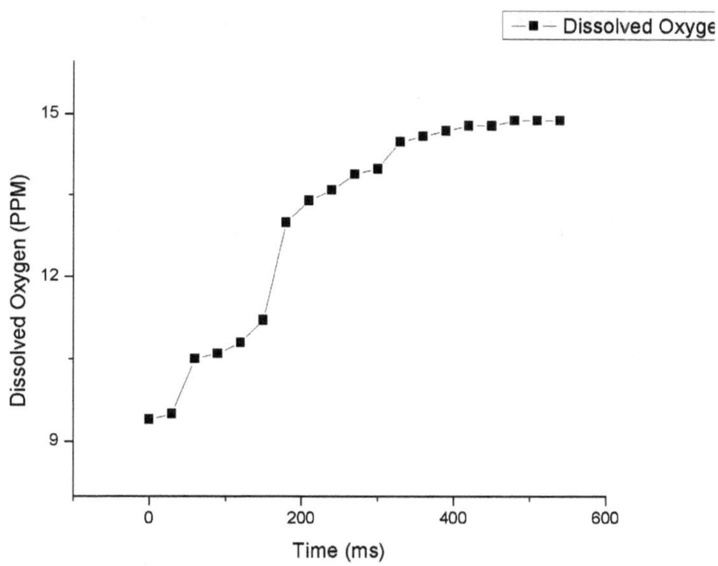

Figure 5.12 Open Loop Response of DO (PPM) Sensor with 10V Input to Pump

Figure 5.11 & 5.12 demonstrates the response of the pump for the 10V Input concerning time. Form these responses its inferred that the DO value increases with repect to time and reaches saturation at 15 PPM for 10V as the input voltage. Table 5.5 represents the DO value response in the aeration tank in the 10V input to the Air pump.

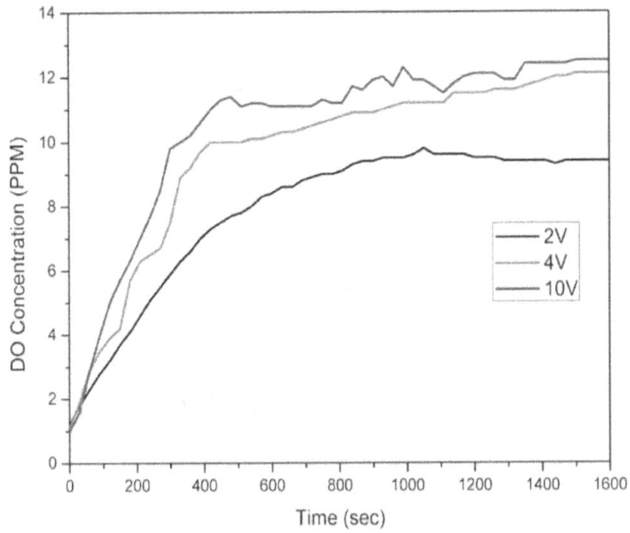

Figure 5.13 Response of Pump for Various Input Voltages

Figure 5.13 epics the variation in the DO concentration during the aeration process by varying the pump voltage in the range of 2V, 4V, and 10V. By changing the pump input voltage, data are collected and used for designing gain values of the PID controller. Figure 5.14 shows the real time setup for DO aeration process.

Figure 5.14 Laboratory Setup for DO Aeration Process

5.4 CONTROLLER DESIGN

5.4.1 PID Controller Design for DO

The real-time PID controller is implemented using LabVIEW. The setpoint of 5 PPM is taken to the three samples, and the PID controls the process. The steady-state is obtained at various load changes of each sample. The PID Controller designed using LabVIEW is tuned using Ziegler Nichole's method, and the gain is changed by noting the system's response.

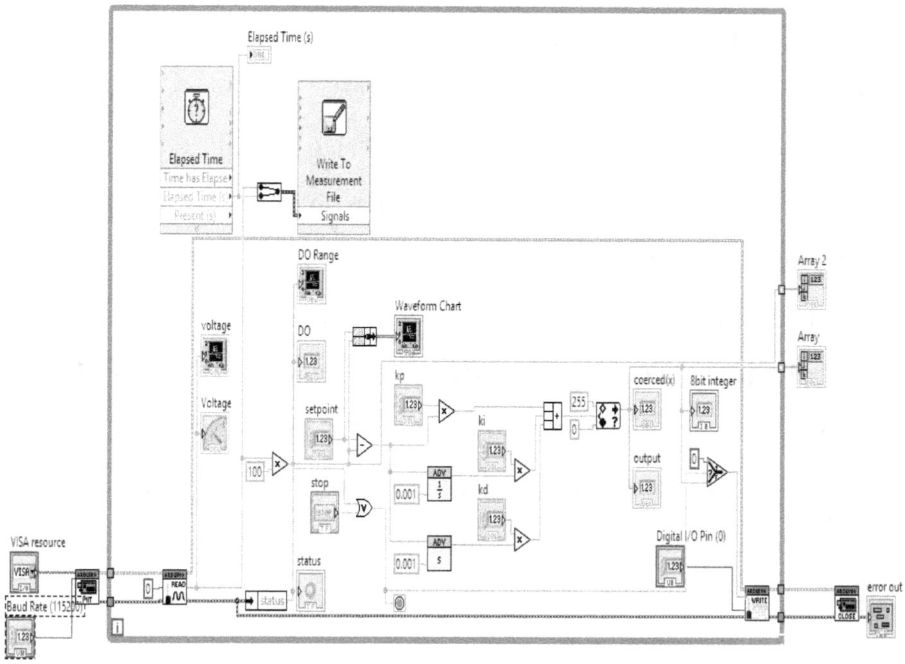

Figure 5.15 LabVIEW Program to Control DO Level Using PID Controller

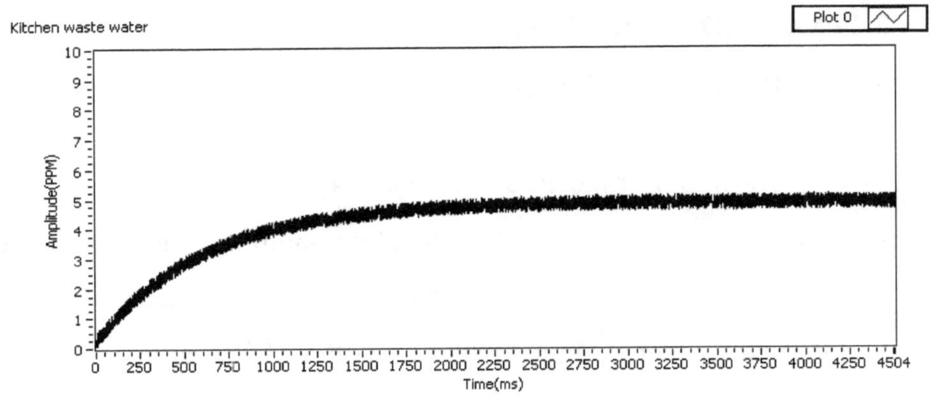

Figure 5.16 Response of DO for Domestic Wastewater

Figure 5.15 shows the design of the LabVIEW program to control DO levels. The design of controllers is always different in real-time implementation. Therefore PID controller gain values are chosen from the trial and error method and its suits for dissolved oxygen concentration set-point tracking. Proportional & Integral controllers are used frequently in the automation industry, especially when quickness of the response is negligible. A control without Derivative mode is used when the system's fast reaction is not needed, and significant disturbances and noise are present during the operation of the process. As the aeration process makes the DO change quickly, Proportional, Integral, and derivative gain very much need for this process.

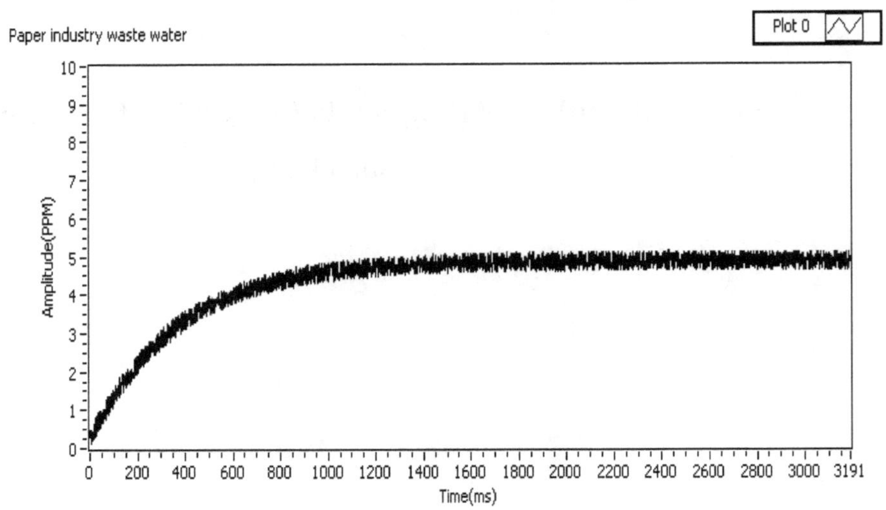

Figure 5.17 Response of DO for Paper Industry Wastewater

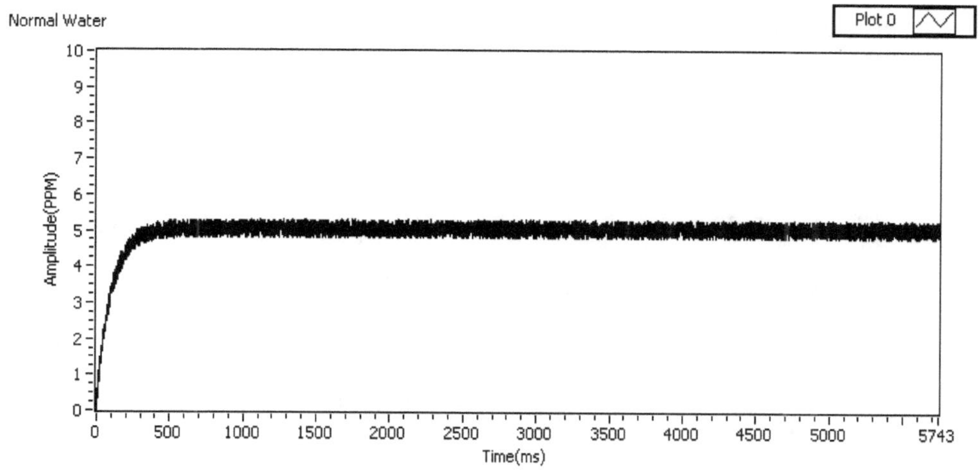

Figure 5.18 Response of DO for Drinking Water

Table 5.6 Settling time of three Different Samples

S. No	Descriptions	Settling Time (ms)
1	Domestic Wastewater	1450
2	Paper Industry Wastewater	1125
3	Normal Water	310

Figure 5.16 describes the DO Control in domestic wastewater. The wastewater must have a minimum of 5 PPM levels of DO concentration as per the literature survey. Hence set point of 5PPM was taken to control the concentration of DO. Figure 5.17 shows the DO control for paper industry wastewater, and the PID controller achieved the setpoint value of 5 PPM within 1000 milliseconds. These experiments are tried out with 30L water. The DO control for normal water is given in Figure 5.18. Comparing all these three results, normal water reacts quickly to reach the set point of 5 PPM. And these experiments were performed multiple times with freshwaters in the setup. The designed controller responses show that the controller can track DO concentration effectively using hybrid variables rather than measuring single

variable-based DO control. Through this hybrid variables-based automation process, much amount of the energy can be saved.

Table 5.6 compares the output response of DO for Domestic Wastewater, Paper Industry Wastewater, and drinking water, respectively. From the response, it has been observed that the time taken to achieve the desire set point is much greater for industrial and domestic wastewater compared to drinking water. Hence it's evident that the aeration process is much required to maintain the dissolved oxygen value.

5.5 CONCLUSION

The industrial effluents and domestic wastewater have been measured with respect to of turbidity and DO concentration. The turbidity sensor and DO sensor were calibrated with the help of a standard solution. The designed turbidity measurement is another useful method to measure colloidal particles of water in fields with a lesser conceptual cost aspect. Many phototransistors were used to enhance the sensitivity of measuring turbidity values. The model-free controller controls the DO concentration effectively using both variables, namely turbidity and DO concentration. Controlling DO level concentration decreases the risk of polluting the land and can cut down many harmful factors. PID controllers responses with DO concentration level for domestic wastewater, industrial effluent, and drinking water were shown. From the answers, it was understood the controller is effectively controlling the DO concentration without any overshoot and undershoot. The real-time PID controller was successfully implemented in the pilot plant. The adaptive controller will be proposed to reduce the settling time of the process.

CHAPTER 6

CONCLUSION AND FUTURE WORK

The experiments were conducted to measure & remove the color from the textile wastewater. The color sensor data is acquired via a NI-DAQ in LabVIEW, and the PID controller is implemented to change the pump by PWM circuit. The implementation of this control algorithm proved to increase the performance of the system by improving the water quality. Flow control made accurate by implementing the PWM input to the pump. For that purpose, the entire process should be done inside the anaerobic chamber, controlled, and monitored effectively by LabVIEW. The filterate quality was tested using SA and PUF bio-reactors where the PUF bioreactor was observed to be the optimal filter model. To ensure safety purposes, the pump was made to stop when the decolorizing efficiency of the filters went beyond 90%. This system can be effectively implemented in any wastewater treatment plant, specifically in all textile industries, to avoid environmental pollution.

Open-loop and the closed-loop response of pH Neutralization are studied and implemented with a real-time PID controller so that the system is physically realizable and works very fast to neutralize pH. The performance of the implemented real time PID controller for pH Neutralization process was found to be highly efficient and reliable.

Dissolved oxygen concentration is measured and controlled with PID controllers output responses for domestic wastewater, industrial effluent, and drinking water. The turbidity sensor and DO sensor were calibrated with the help of a standard solution. The designed turbidity measurement is another useful tool to measure colloidal particles of water in fields with a lesser conceptual cost aspect. Many phototransistors were used to enhance the sensitivity of measuring turbidity values. The model-free controller controls the DO concentration effectively using both variables, namely turbidity and DO concentration. The controlling of DO level concentration decreases the risk of polluting the land and can cut down many harmful factors. PID controllers' output responses with DO concentration level for domestic wastewater, industrial effluent, and drinking water were shown. From the performance analysis, it was understood the controller is effectively controlling the DO concentration without any overshoot and undershoot. The real-time PID controller was successfully implemented in the pilot plant. The adaptive controller will be proposed to reduce the settling time of the process.

The above said implemented system can be further modified and scaled to perform in larger systems. However the conventional control algorithms discussed in this thesis can be replaced with adaptive controllers with control parameters optimized by various optimization techniques

REFERENCES

Abdullah. N. H. S., Karsiti. M. N., & Rosdiazli Ibrahim. (2012). A Review of pH Neutralization Process Control. *4th International Conference on Intelligent and Advanced Systems (ICIAS2012),* 594-598.

Amalendu. P. Ranjan., & James Gomes. (2010). Decoupled Adaptive Control of Glucose and Dissolved Oxygen for Fed-batch Methionine Production Using Linear Reference Model. *American Control Conference Marriott Waterfront, Baltimore, Md, USA,* 5862-5867.

Amir Hajialia., & Gevorg. P. Pirumyan. (2014). Evaluation of Turbidity & Color Removal in Treatment of Wastewater Containing Resistant Pollutants with Ozonation. *International Conference on Environment Systems Science and Engineering*, 8-12.

Andre Felipe Oliveira de Azevedo Dantas., Fabio Araujo de Lima., Andre Laurindo Maitelli., & Gaspar Fontineli Dantas Junior. (2011). Comparative Study of Strategies for Fuzzy Control P & PD applied to a pH plant. *IECON 2011 - 37th Annual Conference of the IEEE Industrial Electronics Society*, 561-521.

Audun Faane., & Sigurd Skogestad. (2004). pH-neutralization: integrated process and control design. *Computers and Chemical Engineering,* 28, 1475–1487.

Ayla Altınten. (2007). Generalized predictive control applied to a pH neutralization process. *Computers and Chemical Engineering,* 31, 1199–1204.

Barathi. S., & Indra Arulselvi. P. (2015). Decolorization, Degradation, and Toxicological Analysis of Textile Dye Effluent by Using Novel Techniques – Review. *International Journal of scientific research and management (IJSRM)*, 3(2), 2118-2136.

Bernt. M. Akesson., Hannu. T. Toivonen., Jonas. B. Waller., & Rasmus. H. Nystrom. (2005). Neural network approximation of a nonlinear model predictive controller applied to a pH neutralization process. *Computers and Chemical Engineering,* 29, 323–335.

Ciprian Vlad., Sergiu Caraman., Daniela Carp., Viorel Mînzu., & Marian Barbu. (2012). Gain Scheduling Control of Dissolved Oxygen Concentration in a Wastewater Treatment Process. *IEEE 20th Mediterranean Conference on Control and Automation*, 860-865.

Daneshvar. N., Rabbani. M., Modirshahla. N., & Behnajady. M. A. (2005). Photooxidative degradation of Acid Red 27 in a tubular continuous-flow photoreactor: Influence of operational parameters and mineralization products. *Journal of Hazardous Materials*, B 118, 155-160.

Davood Shaghaghi., Hossein MonirVaghefi., & Alireza Fatehi. (2013). Generalized Predictive Control of pH neutralization Process Based on Fuzzy Inverse Model. *13th Iranian Conference on Fuzzy Systems (IFSC),* 1-6.

Dr. Alwan. G. M. (2008). pH-Control Problems of Wastewater Treatment Plants. *Al-Khwarizmi Engineering Journal*, 4(2), 37- 45.

Duy Nguyen Tien., Phuong Huy Nguyen., Thi Mai Thuong Duong., & Thu May Duong. (2018). Designing an Adaptive PID Controller for Dissolved Oxygen Control of the Activated Sludge Wastewater Treatment using Hedge Algebras. *International Journal on Future Revolution in Computer Science and Communication Engineering,* 4(5), 177-184.

Estofanero. L., Edwin. R. Garcia., & Claudio. (2019). Predictive Controller Applied to a pH Neutralization Process. *IFAC Papers Online,* 52(1), 202–206.

Flemming buchhol. T., & Mogens kimmel. (1979). Self-tuning Control of a pH-Neutralization Process. *Automatica*, 15, 665-671.

Gomez. J. C., Jutan. A. & Baeyens. E. (2004). Wiener model identification and predictive control of a pH neutralization process. *IEE Proceeding Control Theory Applications.,* 151(3), 329-338.

Han. Y., Brdys. M. A., & Piotrowski. R. (2008). Nonlinear PI control for dissolved oxygen tracking at wastewater treatment plant. *The International Federation of Automatic Control*, 13587-13592.

Hermansson. A. W., & Syafiie. S. (2015). Model predictive control of pH neutralization processes: A review. *Control Engineering Practice,* 45, 98–109.

Hermansson. A. W., Syafiie. S., & Mohd Noor. S. B. (2010). "Multiple Model Predictive Control of Nonlinear pH Neutralization System". 2010 *IEEE International Conference on Industrial Engineering and Engineering Management,* 301-304.

Holenda. B., Domokos. E., Edey. A. R., & Fazakas. J. (2008). Dissolved oxygen control of the activated sludge wastewater treatment process using model predictive control. *Computers and Chemical Engineering,* 32, 1270–1278.

HU Xuemei., HU Yingzhan., & YU Xingzhi .(2011). The Soft Measure Model of Dissolved Oxygen Based on RBF Network in Ponds. *IEEE Fourth International Conference on Information and Computing,* 38-41.

Hua Yin., Peiwen Qiu., Yuange Qian., Zhuwen Kong., Xiaolong Zheng., Zhihua Tang., & Huafang Guo. (2019). Textile Wastewater Treatment for Water Reuse: A Case Study. *Processes*, 1-21.

Javier Gamiz., Yolanda Bolea., Antoni Grau., Juan Gamiz., Francisco Luque., & Juan Miguel Vargas. (2012). Automation of Chlorination Process for Drinking Water Treatment Plant: Control Strategies. *IEEE 10th International Conference on Industrial Informatics,* 337-341.

Karol Błaszkiewicz., Robert Piotrowski., & Kazimierz Duzinkiewicz.(2014). A Model-Based Improved Control of Dissolved Oxygen Concentration in Sequencing Wastewater Batch Reactor. *Studies in Informatics and Control*, 23 (4), 323-332.

Kazimierz Duzinkiewicz., Mietek. A. Brdys., Wojciech Kurek., & Robert Piotrowski. (2009). Genetic Hybrid Predictive Controller for Optimized Dissolved-Oxygen Tracking at Lower Control Level. *IEEE Transactions On Control Systems Technology*, 17(5), 1183-1192.

Kostas. N. Tarchanidis., John. N. Lygouras., Theodore Pachidis., Vassilis Kodogiannis., & Christos. G. Chatziandreoglou. (2006). pH Neutralization Through Internet. *IEEE International Conference on Virtual Environments, Human-Computer Interfaces, and Measurement Systems*, 19-23

Kyu-Hyung Cho., Yeong-Koo Yeff., Jin-Sung Kim., & Seung-tae Koh. (1999). Fuzzy model predictive control of nonlinear pH process. *Korean Journal of Chemical Engineering,* 16(2), 208-214.

Lavanya. C., Rajesh Dhankar., Sunil chhikara., & Sarita sheoran. (2014). Degradation of Toxic Dyes: A Review. *International Journal of Current Microbiology and applied sciences,* 3(6), 189-199.

Liangjin., LuoFei., & XuYuGe. (2009). Wastewater DO Concentration Control through NH4 Prediction Based on Evolutionary Radial Basis Function Neural Network. *IEEE Fifth International Conference on Natural Computation,* 378-381.

Liping Fan., & Kosta Boshnakov. (2010). Fuzzy Logic Based Dissolved Oxygen Control for SBR Wastewater Treatment Process. *IEEE Proceedings of the 8th World Congress on Intelligent Control and Automation*, 4142-4146.

Malgorzata Kabsch-Korbutowicz., & Malgorzata Kutylowska. (2011). Use of artificial intelligence in predicting the turbidity retention coefficient during ultrafiltration of water. *Environment Protection Engineering,* 37, 75-84.

Mat Shah. M. A., & Md Zain. B. D. (2012). Modeling Flexible Plate as an Aerator to Generate Dissolved Oxygen. *IEEE 8th International Colloquium on Signal Processing and its Applications*, 133- 137.

Matthew John Wade., & Reza Katebi. (2002). A Generic Sensor Model For Wastewater Treatment Plant Control. *IEEE International Conference on Control Applications,* 903-908.

Merih Kıvanc., & Mine Dogruer Ozen. (2017). Screening of Fungi for Decolorization of Dye Wastewater. *International Proceedings of Chemical, Biological and Environmental Engineering*, 100, 1-7.

Mohamed Gaberalla., Mohamed Khair Elarafi., & Suhaila Badarol Hisham. (2008). Modeling and Control of pH Neutralization Using Neural Network Predictive Controller. *International Conference on Control, Automation and Systems,* 1196-1199.

Mouedhen. G., Feki. M., De Petris Wery. M., & Ayedi. H. F. (2008). Behaviour of aluminum electrodes in electrocoagulation process. *Journal of Hazardous Materials,* 150, 124-135.

Nio Tiong Ghee., Sivakumar Kumaresan., & Liau Chung Fan. (2002). Fuzzy PID Controller to Control the pH Neutralization Process. *IEEE Student Conference on Research and Development*, 330-334.

Pavanelli. D., & Bigi. A. (2005). Indirect Methods to Estimate Suspended Sediment Concentration: Reliability and Relationship of Turbidity and Settleable Solids. *Biosystems Engineering,* 90(1), 75–83.

Pawlowski. A., Fernández. I., Guzman. J. L., Berenguel. M., Acien. F. G., & Normey Rico. J. E. (2014). Event-based predictive control of pH in tubular photobioreactors. *Computers and Chemical Engineering,* 65, 28–39.

Prado-Rubio. O. A., Jorgensen. S. B., & Jonsson. G. (2012). pH control structure design for a periodically operated membrane separation process. *Computers and Chemical Engineering* 43, 120–129.

Pravin Rose. T., & Glan Devadhas. G. (2019). Detection of pH Neutralization Technique in multiple tanks using ANFIS controller. *Microprocessors and Microsystems*, 72, 102845-102849.

Raynitchka Tzoneva. (2007). Optimal PID Control of the Dissolved Oxygen Concentration in the Wastewater Treatment Plant. *IEEE AFRICON,* 1-6.

Robert Piotrowski., & Adam Skiba. (2015). Nonlinear Fuzzy Control System for Dissolved Oxygen with Aeration System in Sequencing Batch Reactor. *Information Technology and Control,* 182-195.

Shahin Salehi., Mohammad Shahrokhi., & Ali Nejati. (2009). Adaptive nonlinear control of pH neutralization processes using fuzzy approximators. *Control Engineering Practice,* 17,1329–1337.

Shuhua Ma., linkuan Wang., & Yiding Zhao. (2010). Dissolved Oxygen Monitoring and Control System Based on the CDMA Platform. *IEEE International Conference On Computer Design and Applications* (*ICCDA* 2010), 524-527.

Song. S., Yao. J., He. Z. Q., Qiu. J., & Chen. J. (2008). Effect of operational parameters on the decolourization of C.I. Reactive Blue 19 in aqueous solution by ozone enhanced electrocoagulation. *Journal of Hazardous Materials* 152(1), 204-210.

Syafiie. S., Tadeo. F., & Martinez. E. (2007). Model-free learning control of neutralization processes using reinforcement learning. *Engineering Applications of Artificial Intelligence,* 20, 767–782.

Upadhye Priyanka Arun., Sebastian George., & Mobeen. S. A. (2015). "Control of pH Neutralization Process using Fuzzy Logic: A Review" *International Research Journal of Engineering and Technology (IRJET),* 2(3), 1081-1084.

Vincent. J. Turmel., David Williams., & Karl. O. Jones. (1998). Dissolved Oxygen control strategy comparison for an activated sludge. *Ukacc International Conference on Control*, 98, 1102-1105.

Wioletta Przystas., Ewa Zabłocka-Godlewska., & Elzbieta Grabinska-Sota. (2018). Efficiency of decolorization of different dyes using fungal biomass immobilized on different solid supports. *Brazilian Journal of Microbiology,* 49, 285–295.

Xianjun Du., Junlu Wang., Veeriah Jegatheesan & Guohua Sh. (2018). Dissolved Oxygen Control in Activated Sludge Process Using a Neural Network-Based Adaptive PID Algorithm. *Applied Sciences*, 1-21.

Xiao chenn., Anke Xue., Dongliang Peng., & Yunfei Guo. (2014). Modeling of pH neutralization process using fuzzy recurrent neural network and DNA based NSGA-II. *Journal of the Franklin Institute,* 351, 3847–3864.

Xu Zhe., Shouqi Cao., Hak Kyeong Kim., & Sang Bong Kim. (2008). Nonlinear Constrained Predictive Control of Dissolved Oxygen in Bio-reactor. *IEEE Proceedings of the 7th World Congress on Intelligent Control and Automation,* 1522-1526.

Yi Man., Wenhao Shen., Xiaoquan Chen., Zhou Long., & Jean-Pierre Corriou. (2018). Dissolved oxygen control strategies for the industrial sequencing batch reactor of the wastewater treatment process in papermaking industry. *The Royal Society of Chemistry,* 20, 1-10.

Yi Mana., Wenhao Shena., Xiaoquan Chena., & Marie-Noelle Pons. (2017). Control Strategy for Dissolved Oxygen of Paper Mill Activated Sludge Wastewater Treatment Process. *Chemical Engineering Transactions,* Vol. 61, 307-312.

Yingying Gao., Bo Yang., & Qing Wang. (2017). Biodegradation and Decolorization of Dye Wastewater: A Review. *4th International Conference on Environmental Systems Research,* 1-5.

Yuge Xu., Yongtao Zhang., Meijin Lin., & Fei Luo. (2014). Modeling of Dissolved Oxygen concentration in Activated Sludge Process based on Generalized Dynamic Fuzzy Neural Networks. *IEEE*, 4654-4659.

Zanila. M. F., & Hussain. M. A. (2015). Multivariable Adaptive Lyapunov Fuzzy Controller for pH Neutralization Process. *12th International Symposium on Process Systems Engineering and 25th European Symposium on Computer-Aided Process Engineering*. 1643-1648.

Zawadzki. A., & Piotrowski. R. (2012). Nonlinear fuzzy control of the dissolved oxygen in activated sludge processes. *IEEE 17th International Conference on Emerging Technologies & Factory Automation (ETFA 2012),* 1-7.

www.ingramcontent.com/pod-product-compliance
Lightning Source LLC
LaVergne TN
LVHW082353200926
848481LV00012B/3555
* 9 7 9 8 2 3 1 9 5 4 4 1 4 *